How to Live the Holy Life

A Down-to-Earth Look at Holiness

How to Live the Holy Life

A Down-to-Earth Look at Holiness

Copyright 1986
Beacon Hill Press of Kansas City
Kansas City, Missouri

Printed in the United States of America

Stephen M. Miller
Editor

Mary Jo Van Dyne
Editorial Assistant

Jack Mottweiler
Chairman
David Holdren
Stephen M. Miller
Carl Pierce
Gene Van Note
Lyle Williams
Editorial Committee

ISBN: 083-411-1039

Contents

Holy Living:

A Scene from Life

For Rebecca, this is shaping up to be a terrible, horrible, no good, very bad day.

It's Wednesday, her day off from the full-time nursing job. As usual, her husband left her a list of things to do: get the clunker repaired, buy the city stickers for both cars, call the lawn service company about the weeds in the yard . . .

Tonight she's got to go with the pastor's wife on home visitation. She got "hornswoggled" into it, even though she's in charge of the missionary program afterward.

On top of that, her little girl is in bed, trying to get over Asiatic flu. Her young son threw up his Cream of Wheat on the kitchen table—now he's in bed sucking on a thermometer. And Rebecca's not feeling so great herself.

In spite of all this, Rebecca takes a few minutes for devotions over a cup of coffee. It will help take off some of the pressure, she decides. Then she reads Christ's words from the Sermon on the Mount, "You are to be perfect."

"Impossible," she cries right out loud. "Surely He doesn't expect that of me, especially not today."

For the Rebecca in each of us, Jerry Hull will help us see that God's expectations are realistic, and that we really can live holy lives in this unholy, real world.

Chapter 1

When Holiness Meets the Real World

by Jerry D. Hull

Background Scripture: 1 Peter 1:13—2:3

THE MUSCULAR ATHLETE admitted, "Sometimes I'm not sure I even know how to be a holy Christian. All day long I find myself wondering what I need to do to live for Christ."

Most of us are eager to do what's right. The problem is in determining what's right. We don't resist holy living. Rather, we struggle with how to live in order to be holy. All the while we're haunted with the requirement that we must live Christlike lives. We wonder if the expectation is too much.

God, Please Get off My Case!

The pressures of the real world are sometimes hard to deal with. I had one of those days recently. Gary wanted me to talk with Dan and his friends. Audrey wanted a key that was nowhere to be found. Tim wanted advice. Todd wanted information. In the meantime, Dianne kept piling reports and memos on my desk. Colene filled my calendar with appointments.

In addition, correspondence in my letter stack reminds me of many concerns. The Mayor's Human Relations Commission hasn't heard from me for three months. In three weeks Steve wants a 2,000-word article finished. And today, of all days, I begin a three-day retreat in which I must lead five sessions for a group of high-powered professionals.

Demands. Requirements. Obligations. Expectations. Duties. Everyone, it seems, makes claims upon us.

Sometimes we grow weary simply thinking about what everyone wants us to be and do. "Get off my case" is one response we can give to a demanding world. After all, we have only limited time, money, and energy. We can't be all things to all people. We need a little space just to be ourselves.

God, our Heavenly Father, seems to be like everyone else. He, also, has aspirations for us. Once in a while we feel like telling Him to "bug off" and leave us alone. Sometimes we tell Him just that.

We all encounter crushing times. Pressures build. Something must give. I must confess that some days I am so bone weary and so far behind that I wonder if I can carry on. In such times I should whisper a prayer, roll up my sleeves, and redouble my efforts. I know what should be done. Instead, I want to sprawl out on the den floor and take a nap.

How do we respond when everyone, including God, is on our case for more? Or, better? Or, change? Let's be honest about the matter. Sometimes God is the most "pushy" Person in our lives. How's this for pushiness: "You shall be holy, for I am holy" (1 Peter 1:16).*

Everyone has a request. My wife has a dozen requests. My kids want more things. My parents want, and deserve, more of my time. My students want answers and reasons. My local church wants teachers and callers. My work colleagues want a little more, a little sooner. Now, on top of all of this, God wants me TO BE HOLY.

Matthew announced the same demanding request. He recorded Jesus' statement from the Sermon on the Mount, "Therefore you are to be perfect" (Matthew 5:48). We should not be surprised. God has made these sounds for a long while. For example, look at some demands from the first books in the Old Testament:

8

You shall be blameless before the Lord your God *(Deuteronomy 18:13)*.

For I am the Lord, who brought you up from the land of Egypt, to be your God; thus you shall be holy for I am holy *(Leviticus 11:45)*.

You shall consecrate yourselves therefore and be holy, for I am the Lord your God *(Leviticus 20:7)*.

Paul gets in on the act of stating the case for holy living:

Let us cleanse ourselves from all defilement of flesh and spirit, perfecting holiness in the fear of God *(2 Corinthians 7:1)*.

John adds his two bits:

The one who says he abides in Him ought himself to walk in the same manner as He walked *(1 John 2:6)*.

The message comes through, loud and clear. We must go about the business of being holy. But what does "being holy" mean?

He Must Become Number One

Bill and Polly were fortunate people. Life treated them well. They were young, healthy, prosperous, respected, and loved by a close-knit extended family. They owned two special treasures, Billy and Wanda. Billy's wavy hair was fire-engine red; Wanda's was strawberry blonde. You couldn't find a more beautiful set of kids for miles around.

Bill stood among us and sobbed through a testimony. "I hardly slept last night as God talked with me. God asked me if He could have my house and my business and my possessions. I had no trouble saying yes.

"Then God asked me if He could have my kids. I wrestled and wrestled with God. But I was not released until I finally was able to say, 'Yes, God, my kids also. You can even take my kids.'"

Bill, the handsome and successful young father, completed his testimony by telling his friends, "I told God that

I'll serve Him, even if it means letting Him take my kids. I won't let anything keep me from serving Jesus."

I heard Bill's testimony almost 40 years ago. His reckless abandon to live for Jesus became a model that I've never been able to escape. Here was a leading father in our congregation saying that God was first and foremost in his life. Everything else was secondary to his relationship with Jesus.

Bill's testimony reminds me of Jesus' command for holy living:

> You shall love the Lord your God with all your heart, and with all your soul, and with all your mind *(Matthew 22:37)*.

Bill's testimony and life sound a lot like some other radical words of Jesus that help us understand what holy living is about:

> He who loves father or mother more than Me is not worthy of Me; and he who loves son or daughter more than Me is not worthy of Me. And he who does not take his cross and follow after Me is not worthy of Me *(Matthew 10:37-38)*.

Bill illustrated to me, a young boy at the time, a picture of what holy living is about. He taught me that Jesus must be Number One.

Jesus Must Be King

We moderns who live in nations that select leaders by popular elections find king and queen stuff somewhat old-fashioned. We do understand, however, that a "kingdom" refers to a region in which there is only one sovereign.

The king, as sovereign, owns everything in the kingdom. He may use anything in the kingdom for any purpose he wishes. His word is law. At the king's command people are either slaughtered or promoted.

People within a king's domain are referred to as "subjects." Simply, subjects must offer themselves to the king's whims, moods, and fancies, regardless. The wishes, feelings, and concerns of the subjects don't matter because the king is sovereign.

To live holy lives means we must subject ourselves to King Jesus. One BIG PROBLEM develops here—we each want to be the king of our own life, though we don't do well trying to act like kings. We were created to be subjects of King Jesus.

Jesus was a model of yielding to God. His submission to the Father shows how we must submit our lives to Jesus. Paul provided us a portrait of Jesus' submission:

> Although He existed in the form of God, [He] did not regard equality with God a thing to be grasped, but emptied Himself, taking the form of a bond-servant, . . . He humbled Himself by becoming obedient to the point of death, even death on a cross *(Philippians 2:6-8)*.

Jesus acted out submission in the eerie quietness of Gethsemane. Jesus prayed to His Father, "My Father, if it is possible, let this cup pass from Me; yet not as I will, but as Thou wilt" (Matthew 26:39*b*).

Relationships that players have with a coach may help us understand submission to Jesus, as Sovereign. Recently I learned of a football team that illustrates our stubborn independence to be our own king. The team members know the game. They practice hard. They are fast, agile, and well-trained players.

One serious problem remains—they seldom win a game. Why? The problem appears to be the presence of too many "coaches." Almost every one of these talented guys claims to know the game and game strategies better than the coach. Failure to yield to the leadership of the coach has produced a sorry season.

A team that fails to acknowledge the authority of the coach is like a team trying to run 11 different plays at once. A winning team, in contrast, is composed of athletes who voluntarily yield to the instructions of the coach.

When we join Coach Jesus' team, we allow Him to call the plays, assign the positions, select the schedule, determine all of the practices, and decide on postseason awards.

Holy living means that we acknowledge Jesus as the ultimate Coach (King) of our lives.

We Are for God's Use

I just finished reading the Books of Exodus and Leviticus. Frankly, much of the material is boring. For example, why all the fuss over the shape, size, and materials for the Tabernacle? Why would God demand that we "read-the-Bible-through-in-a-year-folks" with all the intricate details regarding wave offerings, burnt offerings, heave offerings, grain offerings, sin offerings, and . . .

I was amused by God's instructions to Moses when he consecrated Aaron and Aaron's sons (see Leviticus 8). God left nothing to chance. Moses slaughtered a ram. He took some of the ram's blood and put a drop on the lobe of Aaron's right ear. Another drop he put on the thumb of Aaron's right hand. Then, apparently for good measure, Moses put a drop of the ram's blood on the big toe of Aaron's right foot. Now, tell me, why all the fuss?

I don't know for sure why all the fuss. But I do know that after all the rituals of consecration, Moses and Aaron were different. As Moses and Aaron left the tent, the glory of the Lord appeared to all the people. Then the fire of the Lord consumed the offering. The scripture writer declared, "When all the people saw it, they shouted and fell on their faces" (Leviticus 9:24).

In God's scheme, every possible caution is taken to purify God's people and set them aside for His use. In a way, God wants us to be containers worthy of His glory and grace. We are to be containers for pouring out God's presence and power, not for selfish hoarding. We realize the power, glory, and presence of God as we begin to serve Him.

Howard taught me a lesson on what it means to be used for God's purposes. I met him in some door-to-door visitation work. A few weeks later, the Lord prompted me to go by Howard's house. Howard and I sat at his kitchen table and talked about work, the local church, and the Lord. Soon it was apparent that he wanted to accept Jesus as his personal Savior. That night, the Lord used my lips and my Bible to speak to Howard. For me, few joys rival being used of God in this way. Someone has correctly observed, "We realize the power of God to the degree we are willing to be used by Him."

Holy living means that we become like the Sea of Galilee and not like the Dead Sea. These two bodies of water have many things in common. They are both in the same region of the world. They both have sources for supply of fresh water. They both have firm banks to contain the water drained into them.

One major difference prevails, however. The Sea of Galilee receives water and PASSES IT ON. The Dead Sea, in contrast, has no means for passing the water on for other purposes. As a result, the Dead Sea is just that, dead.

In the tradition of the Sea of Galilee, we discover holy living as we allow Jesus' love to flow through us in behalf of others.

We Are Who We Are in Jesus

Aldous Huxley, in *Brave New World,* proposed that we produce human beings that know their place and gladly keep in their place. He reasoned that through genetic engineering we should reproduce people according to the types of jobs that need to be accomplished in society. Huxley's world would have, for example, ditchdiggers that would be happy with their task. They would not aspire to be tractor operators. At the same time, tractor operators would not aspire to be draftsmen who would design and build tractors. In other words, everyone would have his place and everyone would be happy in his place.

Few of us wish for Huxley's type of society. We don't want to remain in a constant state. Rather, we push ourselves to reach new levels of achievement. We strive to improve ourselves. Jesus becomes our partner in helping us discover who and what we are created to be.

Reaching our potential forces us to consider what it means to be holy like God is holy. Let's learn well that being holy is by God's grace—not because of our efforts or smarts. Simply stated, one aspect of being holy is being who we are in Jesus.

Recently we celebrated Bethany's seventh birthday. My bright niece was a star for her special occasion. In the supporting cast was her five-year-old brother, Dean. Bethany and Dean reminded me of a truth about holy living. I don't mean to claim that my niece and nephew are always little angels. Sometimes they are not, regardless of what their grandparents say. What I do mean is that Bethany and Dean make being a child seem so easy, which indeed it is. They don't strain at the job. They don't have posters tacked around the house reminding them to be children. Without effort or struggle they act out who they are—children.

No one requires them to laugh, or to speak with open candor. Their parents don't have written rules that they are to be spontaneous. Bethany and Dean are just naturally fascinated with the wonder of everyday things. They giggle and rave over kittens, and worms, and soft mud, and other mysteries.

Bethany and Dean act out who they are. They are not phonies. They don't act like something they "ain't." They are just kids through and through.

Holy living is more than keeping rules, or playing roles. Holy living is more than rigidly controlling emotions, motions, and tongues. Holy living is simply living out who we

14

are in Jesus. We're not holy because we intend to be perfect. We're not holy because we are 100% disciplined, 100% of the time. We're holy because we are living out what God has redeemed us to be—kids in His kingdom.

Kids don't struggle to be kids—they just do what comes naturally. In the same way, we can't be holy by simply trying to be holy. We're holy by His grace, alone. Paul says it so well:

> For by grace you have been saved through faith; and that not of yourselves, it is the gift of God; not as a result of works, that no one should boast. For we are His workmanship, created in Christ Jesus for good works, which God prepared beforehand, that we should walk in them *(Ephesians 2:8-10).*

---

*All Scripture quotations in this chapter are from the *New American Standard Bible.*

Sanctification:

A Scene from Life

Sarah is a confused and frustrated Christian.

On her way home after church one Sunday she turned to her husband and quipped, "One of these days that preacher is going to say something about entire sanctification that I'll understand. Will you be sure to wake me when he does?"

Sarah is confused because she doesn't understand what it means to be sanctified wholly.

And she's frustrated because she's been told she needs it.

So how's she supposed to find it when she doesn't know what "it" is? Is she supposed to slowly grow *up* into spiritual maturity, or abruptly plunge *down* into the cleansing wave? Should she forsake the past, or build on its foundation?

"It'll cleanse your bent to sinning," she's told. "But aren't we all bent to some degree, and subject to temptation?" she asks.

Sarah reminds us that if we can't explain our Christian beliefs in simple English that everyone can understand, then we really don't know what we believe and certainly can't share it with anyone else.

John T. Seamands knows what the Bible says about entire sanctification. For Sarah, and for us, he explains it in plain English.

Chapter 2

What Must I Do?

by John T. Seamands

Background Scripture: Romans 12:1-2; 1 Thessalonians 4:3-8; 5:23-24

THERE ARE SOME who declare that we simply grow into the experience of entire sanctification. They say, "Just give me time. Let me grow. After a while I will be more like a saint." All this sounds good, but it ignores the facts both of Scripture and of general Christian experience. It is a false and dangerous idea.

The truth of the matter is, there are many who were much better Christians shortly after their conversion than they are right now. Why? Because they have not sought to be filled with the Spirit, and as a result have settled down to a halfhearted Christian life. They have been drifting—not growing.

Now there is a certain sense in which we do grow *toward* the experience of the fullness of the Holy Spirit—that is, there is often a process or series of minor crises that leads to the final event of the infilling. Most of us have to *grow up* to a certain place in our Christian lives where we are able to see the need of a deeper work of cleansing and are able to make a more complete surrender of ourselves to Christ.

Perhaps we ought to *grow down* rather than *grow up* to this place of readiness. For the truth of the matter is that not many of us grow gradually and steadily. We are too stubborn and self-centered for that.

God has to bring us *down*, again and again, with crisis after crisis. He has to let us get knocked down, to let us try and fail perhaps several times, until we finally are so utterly desperate that we come to the absolute end of all our own resources and strength. We discover that we are not just sinners, but sin itself, and that in us "dwelleth no good thing." We realize that all our

17

working and striving are as filthy rags, tainted with the subtle evil called self-glorification.

Then in sheer desperation we give up, and make the surrender, and cast ourselves upon the grace of God. If we think that comes about by pleasant and gradual growth, we are sadly mistaken.

Surrender Your Self

Why does the Christian faith place so much emphasis on self-surrender? Simply because the unsurrendered self is the cause of all our spiritual problems. Just as the fingers are rooted in the hand, so our sins are rooted in the palm of the unsurrendered self. Why does a man steal? To gain something for the self. Why does a man lie? To protect the self. Why does a man get jealous? Something is getting ahead of the self. Why does a man think evil thoughts? To gain pleasure for the self.

Take the little word *SIN.* Right in the middle of the word is the letter *I.* It is the unsurrendered ego, the I, that is the root of our problems.

The unsurrendered self is manifested in many different forms. Sometimes it manifests itself in *self-seeking.* The individual, instead of seeking first the kingdom of God and His righteousness, seeks his own pleasure, position, plans, and prestige.

Sometimes the unsurrendered ego manifests itself in *self-love.* The individual, instead of loving God supremely and his neighbor as himself, is actually in love with himself. He thinks more highly of himself than he ought to think and becomes proud. A university professor was so conceited and infatuated with himself that the students jokingly referred to him as "a self-made man who worshiped his creator."

The unsurrendered ego sometimes manifests itself in *self-assertion.* The individual likes to be the center of the group. He likes to dominate the conversation. He likes to talk about himself, where he has been, and what he has accomplished. He frequently uses the personal pronoun "I."

When my brother was working on his master's thesis at Hartford, Conn., some years ago, he rented a typewriter from a local agent. As the man was setting up the typewriter in the apartment, he said to my brother, "You know, the letter on the keyboard that we have to replace more often than any other is the letter *I*. The reason for this," he went on to explain, "is not so much because people use this letter more than any other, but when they use it, they strike the key so hard!"

At times the unsurrendered self is manifested by *self-indulgence*. The individual is motivated by desire. This may lead to excess, gluttony, enslaving habits, or even immorality.

Self-justification is another characteristic of the unsurrendered ego. The person finds it difficult to admit that he was mistaken. He is slow to apologize. He constantly seeks to justify his actions and to vindicate his position.

Then there is *self-sufficiency*. The individual, instead of relying wholly on the resources and grace of God, depends on his own wisdom, his own ability, his own efforts.

A little girl was singing to herself in the living room of the house one day, while her mother was working in the kitchen. It was an old, familiar song, but this must have been the revised version. The mother smiled as she overheard the daughter singing, "Count your blessings, name them one by one, and it will surprise the Lord what you have done!" Self-sufficiency!

Then again, the unsurrendered self is manifested by *self-will*. Perhaps this is the crux of the matter. The individual, instead of seeking God's will in every decision and area of life, often desires to go his own way. In his wonderful book titled *The Great Divorce*, C. S. Lewis suggests that in the last analysis there are only two groups of people in the world. The first group comprises those who say to God, "Not my will, but Thine be done." The second group are those to whom God eventually has to say, "Not My will, but thine be done. You wanted to have your way; all right, you can have it—forever." And Lewis suggests that when God eventually and decisively says this to any man, that is hell.

The self is usually the last thing we are willing to surrender. It's easy to *give to* Christ, to give *things;* it's hard to *give up* to Christ, to present *ourselves*. We usually are willing to give anything to Christ—money, possessions, even service—

everything but our own selves. I remember a layman in India who confessed before the congregation, "All these years I have given my offerings faithfully to the Lord, but I have never really given myself." A young single missionary, who went out to India to pastor an English-speaking congregation in a large city, said in a retreat one day, "I had left my home and loved ones, a good job and a fine salary, to come to India to work for God, but until today I had not surrendered myself."

There are basically two patterns of life: one revolving around self as the center, and the other revolving around God as the center. The New Testament symbolically speaks of these patterns as "the old man" and "the new man." All of the events and stuff of which life is made fall into one or the other of these patterns. Indeed, to some extent in unsurrendered hearts these patterns exist simultaneously, overlapping.

In his book titled *The Spirit of Holiness,* Dr. Everett Cattell illustrates this common spiritual condition by passing a horseshoe magnet under a sheet of paper on which have been sprinkled iron filings. Looking from above one cannot see the magnet, but one can tell the location of its poles by the behavior of the filings, which instantly arrange themselves around the poles and form two overlapping patterns. "In the lives of converted men," suggests Dr. Cattell, "there are still two great poles—self and God. All of the particles that go to make up life, group themselves around these two poles in patterns of life which are partially self-centered and partially God-centered. It is conceivable that the particles where the patterns overlap have a hard time making up their minds as to which pole to obey."

We must be cleansed of self-centeredness. This duality of pattern must go out of existence. The self as a pole apart from God must yield up its aloofness, its separateness, its enmity against God, its independent sovereignty, by an act of utter surrender. It must move over and become hidden with Christ in God. The self then continues to live, but it lives in God. The poles are now—so to speak—identical, and the pattern of life is one—integrated.

This is most concisely and intriguingly expressed by Paul

in his oft quoted words, "I have been crucified with Christ; it is no longer I who live, but Christ who lives in me; and the life I now live in the flesh I live by faith in the Son of God, who loved me and gave himself for me" (Galatians 2:20, RSV).

There is the story of a man who was glancing over the obituary section of the morning newspaper, when, to his surprise, he found his own name in the list. He looked again. Sure enough, the initials, name, and address were all correct. He was reported as dead. At first he laughed over the matter, but soon the telephone began ringing, as many of his stunned friends sought to inquire about his sudden death. Finally, he became irritated and called up the newspaper editor. "Sir," he said, "you have reported my death in the morning paper, but I'm very much alive. It's causing a lot of confusion among my friends. I demand you set this right!"

The editor was at first apologetic, but then in a flash of inspiration he said, "Don't worry, Sir. I'll make things right. Tomorrow I'll put your name in the birth column!"

This is a spiritual parable. If we die out to the old carnal self, then suddenly we will find ourselves alive in Christ—alive as never before. For after the crucifixion comes the resurrection. The old self dies and a new self arises. We put our names in the death column and immediately we find them placed in the birth column.

A note of warning needs to be sounded at this point. The crucifixion of the old self that we have been emphasizing cannot be brought about by the individual himself. That is, self cannot crucify itself. It is irrevocably opposed to its own crucifixion. The only thing the individual can do is to *become willing* for the self to be crucified by the Holy Spirit, who alone is the Executioner. But when we are willing, then we find He is able.

Receive the Fullness of the Spirit

The full surrender of the self is not an end in itself. It is merely cleaning the channel so that the Spirit may give himself in His fullness.

This must not, however, be interpreted as a form of celestial bargaining, whereby we give our all and in exchange He gives His all. By a full surrender we are not in any sense making ourselves worthy to receive the fullness of the Spirit. No one is worthy, but all Christians are eligible. This is God's gift, and it is for the asking. Jesus said, "If you then, who are evil, know how to give good gifts to your children, how much more will the heavenly Father give the Holy Spirit to those who ask him!" (Luke 11:13, RSV). All we need to do is ask the Holy Spirit who lives in us to take full control and sanctify and fill.

It was shortly after my wife and I arrived in India to begin our missionary career that the Japanese attacked Pearl Harbor and drew the United States into World War II. Within a few months, Japanese forces had advanced to the borders of India, and the U.S. ambassador was urging all American citizens to evacuate. My wife and six-month-old daughter returned by troop transport to the United States, but I remained behind on the field. It was two years and seven months before we were reunited.

During the long period of separation my wife and I suffered many hours of loneliness. My wife wrote to me regularly, but in those war years mail was slow and the censorship was strict. Often whole sections of a letter were cut out. At times she mailed me a parcel with some special gift as a token of her love. On one occasion while I was holding special revival meetings in Calcutta, a thief broke into the parsonage and, among other household articles, stole my best suit and fountain pen. When my wife heard of the loss, with her meager savings she bought me a new suit and fountain pen, and mailed them out to me in India. I was, of course, delighted to receive the gift. But I wrote to her and said, "Dearest, I thank you for all your letters that assure me of your love and prayers. I thank you for all the parcels, and especially for this most recent one. But, Darling, I am getting to the place where I am not satisfied with just letters and parcels. I long for you and you alone. If I could just look into your face and hold you in my arms, that would be worth more than thousands of letters and parcels. The next time you send me a parcel, just wrap yourself up and come out!"

There came a time in my spiritual life when I had to say much the same thing to the Holy Spirit. I said in my heart,

"Lord, I thank You for all Your gifts—for forgiveness, for peace, for comfort, and strength. But, Lord, I want more than just gifts. I want only You. I want You to permeate and fill every part of my being."

We must desire the Lord more than anything else in the whole world. We must want Him and Him alone.

Finally we must receive the Holy Spirit in His fullness *by faith*. Peter said before the council in Jerusalem, "And God who knows the heart bore witness to them, giving them the Holy Spirit just as he did to us; and he made no distinction between us and them, but cleansed their hearts *by faith*" (Acts 15:8-9, RSV, italics added).

Faith is merely taking God at His word, letting my whole weight down on His promises. He assures us that the gift of the Holy Spirit is for all; that He gives the Holy Spirit to those who ask Him; that if we shall ask anything in His name, He will grant it. So I say in my heart, "Lord, I know what You say is true. I now ask to be filled with the Spirit, and I believe that You fill me at this moment. Thank You, Lord."

Since this experience is entered into by faith, it can happen in our lives anytime, anywhere, when we ask and believe.

In a certain church I was giving a series of messages on the subject of the Holy Spirit. A young housewife, a sincere child of God, became hungry for the fullness of the Spirit.

One morning, all alone in the house, she was working in the kitchen. In her mind, however, she was meditating and praying. Suddenly she lifted her eyes and said aloud, "Lord, the preacher said we can receive the baptism with the Holy Spirit by faith. This, I see, is in accordance with Your Word. So, Lord, right here and now I ask You to fill me with the Holy Spirit, and I believe You do." In the evening service she stood and testified that she had the inner assurance that the Holy Spirit had filled her. It happened while she was in the kitchen, washing the breakfast dishes!

A few years ago, at a quiet retreat for preachers and laymen in New York state, I delivered the same series of messages on the Holy Spirit. At the end of the first session, time was given for questions and discussion. The ministers became involved in the theological pros and cons of the subject. Suddenly a layman, whose first name was Sam, interrupted the discussion and called out. "I don't follow all this theological jargon. All I know is that I need the fullness of the Holy Spirit. Tell me how I can find it." So I briefly outlined the steps of self-surrender and faith.

When the evening session was over, the leader of the retreat explained that we would now begin a period of silence until the morning devotional period. He also informed us that on our way out we should pick up a card containing the name of one of the persons present at the retreat. We were to pray for that person in particular before retiring for the night.

Immediately I said in my heart, "Lord give me Sam as my prayer partner." When I picked up my card and looked at the name it read "Sam ———." Coincidence, you say. But that would be difficult in a stack of approximately 100 cards. I felt it was Providence. I went to my room and prayed earnestly for Sam, that he might be filled with the Spirit.

In the morning we all gathered for corporate, silent devotions. At the end of the period, Sam jumped to his feet and said excitedly, "I could hardly wait for the silence to be broken. I am bursting to share the good news with you. Last night the Lord filled me with the Holy Spirit. I asked and believed, and the Lord answered my prayer."

It happened while he was taking a shower!

I remember in my own life, when I was a student at Asbury College in Wilmore, Ky., how I first received the fullness of the Spirit. I had been a Christian for about two years and had started out very zealously in my Christian life. But then I seemed to hit a plateau. I was making little progress spiritually.

I was deeply distressed at the discovery of certain attitudes and desires in my heart that were clearly contrary to the Spirit of Christ. I was a divided person; there was civil war within. The doctrine of the Holy Spirit and sanctification was not new to me. I had been reared in the Wesleyan tradition. All I needed was to appropriate the truth personally and turn doctrine into experience.

Then one morning, sitting alone at the desk in my private

devotions, I prayed silently within myself, "Lord, You said, 'Blessed are those who hunger and thirst for righteousness, for they shall be satisfied.' Well, I'm hungry now. I'm thirsty. I want to be cleansed and filled with the Spirit more than anything else. Lord, fulfill Your promise now. I believe." At that moment I felt as if I had had a good bath. I felt clean all over. And there was the assurance that the Holy Spirit had taken possession of my being.

Sad to say, I haven't always been faithful to the Master. There was a time when I miserably failed my Lord and lost the assurance of His fullness. But the Spirit was faithful in His ministry of conviction and discipline and brought me back to the place of full surrender and faith. The assurance of His fullness is real today.

These then are the steps to the Spirit-filled life. Surrender yourself completely to His will and die to the old self. Receive Him in His fullness by faith. Realize that it is God's intention to fill you with His Spirit. Make it your intention to be filled. Then the promise will pass into fulfillment in your life and Pentecost will be as real to you as it was to the disciples in the Upper Room at Jerusalem.

From *On Tiptoe with Love,* by John T. Seamands. Copyright 1971 by Beacon Hill Press of Kansas City, Kansas City, Mo. Used by permission.

Holy Security:
A Scene from Life

Linda is having a terrible week. And it all started with the pastor's sermon.

Rev. Small's name is indicative of his theological insight. Last Sunday, this young pastor preached a vivid message of warning to his sanctified church members.

"Just because you're sanctified," he bellowed, "don't think you got it made. You ain't home free yet."

With carefully orchestrated fervor and pulpit-pounding sincerity he proceeded to explain that all sanctified folk are in danger every waking second of losing not only their sanctification, but their salvation as well.

"You can't lose your sanctification without your salvation tagging along. Once you're sanctified, the two become Siamese twins joined at the heart."

Poor Linda.

She hadn't thought she was home free, but neither did she think she was picnicking by a missile silo during a nuclear attack.

There's good news for Linda, and we'll let Keith Drury deliver it.

Chapter 3

Secure and Growing

by Keith Drury

Background Scripture: John 10:27-30; 1 Peter 1:3-5; 1 John 1:5-7

SINCE AN ENTIRELY SANCTIFIED PERSON can live above willful sin, some have wondered if this work of God in a person's heart makes him eternally secure.

They reason that he never will sin again so he will never be lost. This is not true. There is no spiritual height or strength of grace from which it is not possible to fall and finally become lost. Sadly, there is much evidence around us illustrating spiritual "shipwreck."

Security is a relative matter. For instance, I am sitting on a chair as I type these words. Unless I am overtaken by dizziness or severe sickness, my chances of falling out of this chair are slight. However, if I stand on it, especially on the edge of the chair, I am more likely to fall—that is, I am less secure. If the chair is placed on top of a table as I stand on it, my security is further jeopardized. Preposterous as it would be, if I were to stand on the chair while it is perched in the towering tree outside my window, I would be much less secure than sitting here in my office. Security is a relative thing—a person may be more or less secure, depending on where he is and what he is doing.

So it is with the security of believers. Our security is a relative matter. We may be more secure or less secure, depending on where we are and what we decide to do.

There are two extremes here. On one hand there are those who insist on an unconditional security, no matter what. These argue that wherever I am, whatever I do, and regardless of the extent of my rebellion, I continue to be a part of God's family. They say, "Once a son, always a son." On the other hand, some argue that it is not only possible, but even likely, that a believer will fall, resulting in a curious "eternal insecurity." Neither extreme is sound teaching.

As usual, truth is frequently found in the middle of the road. A believer should not ignore the possibility of becoming an easy target for the devil's devices and then falling. But the chances of a believer unwittingly falling from grace are not so high that we need to live in crippling daily fear.

Sanctification and Backsliding

It is possible for a believer to fully consecrate his entire life to God, and then, in faith, receive God's cleansing and power. This is the event of entire sanctification. But the daily walk of the sanctified life must follow the event or experience.

What happens when a person walking in this way does not obey one of the promptings of the Spirit?

For example, Beverly had lived a dedicated Christian life for years before she attended a ladies' retreat where the idea of entire sanctification was presented. She recognized that the one area of "holdout" for her was her unwillingness to witness for Christ to her unsaved friends at work. At the retreat she recognized the reason for her unwillingness to witness. She was more concerned about what her fellow employees thought of her than she was for the spread of the gospel. Some of her associates did not even know she was a Christian.

At the closing service of the retreat, Bev made a total dedication of herself to the Lord and, in faith, received His cleansing and power. She promised to make at least one attempt to share her faith every week from then on. New spiritual vigor came to Beverly during the next several months. Everyone seemed to notice "Bev's renewal." Then Christmas came. With the change of routine, and a vacation trip to her parents, she began to slack off on her commitment. The Lord would prompt her to say something to an unsaved associate at work, and she would willfully resist the idea until the opportunity passed.

Within a few weeks her newly begun habit of a daily time alone with God became less meaningful. Finally whole weeks went by without a day of Bible reading and prayer. Church services became dry and uninteresting to her. She noticed that her old habit of criticizing certain people at church was beginning to return. By Easter, Beverly had to admit that the power she once knew was gone. She still felt she was a believer, but the zest and thrill she associated with the "sanctified life" was gone. She was sliding back, and she knew it.

What will happen to Beverly? Where will she go from here? There are three possibilities:

First, she might continue her slide into further disobedience. Refusing to witness when the Lord prompted had been followed by a drying up of personal devotions, which was soon followed by the return of her critical spirit. Unless Bev stops the slide, she may continue on back toward her old life. This will lead her into outright rebellion against God, and eventual lostness.

Second, and perhaps more likely, Beverly may settle into a state of spiritual lukewarmness, going through the motions at church, but not experiencing the vitality of total surrender. Many in our churches today fall into this second category. They once tasted of the life of total commitment for a period, then they began taking things off the altar of total consecration. Now they live on a plateau of lukewarmness.

Third, Beverly may respond to her realization that she is sliding back with the biblical response to disobedience—repentance. She may confess she has lost power, and recommit her all to Jesus, receiving His cleansing and power again. The sanctified life is maintained the same way it is obtained—by consecration and faith. This is a daily matter, and the life is maintained to the extent to which there is continual daily consecration and a sustained faith.

Sanctification and Security

While backsliding at any stage of growth must always be considered a present danger, we must on the other hand avoid becoming insecure.

A person who constantly lives in obedience to God is totally secure as long as he continues to walk in obedience. This is a relative security. Security is relative to obedience.

The question relating to the person living the sanctified life is, "Will the entirely sanctified person be more likely to obey Christ?" The answer to this is an unequivocal, "Yes!" Thus, the entirely sanctified person can be said to be more secure. He is not unconditionally secure; but as long as he walks in obedience, there need be no fear of falling.

God is not seeking an opportunity to "bounce" believers out of His family. Like a Father, He tenderly encourages, corrects, and chastens His children. If our lives are heading in the wrong direction, He nudges, rebukes, and delivers sometimes painful discipline in an attempt to awaken us and straighten us out. If we "despise" or rebel against this chastening and walk out of His home in rebellion, it is then we forfeit the grace He so freely gave to us.

The crux of the entire matter is, "Am I obeying all known leadings of the Lord?" If I am, there is no need to worry about security. If I am not, then I should worry about the level of my obedience, not security. Security is not the central issue—it is obedience.

Continual Growth

We who speak much about sanctification sometimes appear to emphasize the event of entire sanctification more than the life following this event. This is unfortunate. Of course, the life must have an initiation, thus the emphasis on being cleansed at one time. But the *continual* life of holiness is the central issue in all we have discussed.

The relationship of the wedding to married life is a parallel example. The wedding is the initiation of married life. It is a significant occasion, to be remembered throughout a person's entire life. But if a bride or groom expects to continually live in a wedding-day atmosphere, they will soon be disappointed. Marriage is life lived out in light of the wedding-day commitment.

Entire sanctification must not be viewed as something done "way back then," but as a life here-and-now—in the trenches of life. It is not a static life—you have arrived and are merely sitting around waiting to be taken to heaven. It is a life of active service to the Lord. It is expandable. Further spiritual growth is the inevitable result. While the entirely sanctified person possesses love, compassion, joy, peacefulness, humility, and patience of the same quality as Jesus, the quantity of them is expandable.

Spiritual Dryness

Why in the world would a book on holiness deal with the topic of spiritual dryness? Doesn't the Lord eliminate any possibility of dryness in the life of anyone who is entirely sanctified? Isn't the life of holiness one of constant bubbling and joy in one's soul?

To say the possibilities of spiritual dryness are gone for the sanctified would be untrue. Almost every person testifying to sanctification will honestly admit that there are times when God seems farther away, daily study of the Word seems insipid, and church services leave the individual unmoved and bored. What has happened? Is the work of sanctification lost?

Such spiritual dryness results from several causes. *Disobedience* could be one cause. It is possible that God is urging the believer to move forward to a new area—say, being more generous in giving to God's work—and that he is resisting the idea. This resistance to moving forward will promptly dry up the soul of a sanctified believer. The sanctified life prospers in proportion to our obedience to His known leadings. Any resistance or foot-dragging will divert our lives into a plateau of spiritual dryness from which the only return is repentance and renewed commitment.

However, resistance to the Lord's will is not the only cause of spiritual dryness. Many sincere believers have *cast away their faith* that the Lord had sanctified them fully when they hit the first dry plain in their Christian walk. Assuming that the sanctified life is one of continual joy and celebration, they figured that when things got difficult they had lost it all. So they gave up.

A great season of *temptation* can bring on a period of spiritual dryness. We can experience an assault from the tempter with such vengeance, and for so long a season, that our wrestling against evil leaves us spiritually wrung out.

Another cause is *spiritual burnout.* Christian workers are especially prone to this malady. It is possible to be so involved in church work, camps, retreats, evangelistic teams, counseling, and a million other spiritual activities that spiritual exhaustion results.

Physical burnout is another cause of spiritual dryness. A sanctified mother of three, with low iron, who is holding down a full-time job, carrying several responsibilities at church, and sleeping five hours per night will naturally be tired and bored in church services. Her heart will not leap at the idea of giving another night of her week to go soul winning. Is she still sanctified? Yes. Likely she does not need to go to the altar as much as she needs to go to bed!

The life of holiness is not based upon feelings. To be sure, a life of total submission has feelings associated with it. But reliance on feelings will bring discouragement.

If it has been a general pattern of your life to be somewhat "blue" on Mondays, entire sanctification will not necessarily make your Mondays bright and exciting. One man was troubled because every spring he became discontented, preoccupied, and yearned to quit his job. Only after reflection did he discover that during the first several years of his married life he had moved every single spring. His uneasiness was a result of this natural "cycle of life." Entire sanctification did not change his urge to do something different in the springtime.

It is important to determine the cause of spiritual dryness in the sanctified believer's life. If it is caused by willful resistance to the Lord, repentance is the only cure. But, if it is caused by physical or spiritual burnout, an assault of the tempter, or a natural cycle of life, we should be careful to recognize the reason for our "dryness" and not cast away our faith.

Continual Consecration

At the initial event of our entire sanctification we consecrate all to God—our entire future, time, talent, money, reputation—everything. When these are surrendered to the Lord, He is free to do His work of entire sanctification.

1. Usually there follows a period of joy and excitement as the sanctified believer now walks in full obedience to everything he clearly recognizes as God's will. It can be said that the believer's *life* is in harmony with all his known *light* from God.

2. But the sanctified life is not static. There is growth and expansion. How does this occur? God moves His light! In the midst of our living in total submission to all the past leadings of God, He leads again. He moves His light forward to reveal things He wants me to put off. They are not sin in themselves (yet, they may become sin if I refuse to lay them aside). Usually they are things of "second best" nature—items or practices not sinful, but nevertheless they are weights that slow me down in serving the Lord.

Obviously, these are very personal and can never be applied to others. When God moves His light forward, He often prompts us to lay aside particular things to make us more effective in serving Him. In this way the sanctified person experiences conviction.

The light also reveals new tasks and habits the Lord leads the believer to "put on." Perhaps the Lord convicts the sanctified believer to begin a weekly habit of soul winning, or double tithing, or doing deeds of mercy for the poor. Again if the sanctified believer rebels against the Lord's guidance, sin will result.

3. The sanctified believer has settled the question—he will obey the Master whatever the cost. The natural result of this process of continual sanctification will be a stepping forward into the full brightness of God's revealed light.

This is the continuous walk of holiness. It is "walking in the light!" It is the natural expanding process of becoming more like Jesus. At the moment of entire consecration the issue was settled—my will was and is submitted completely to Jesus. Yet, there will be multitudes of challenging situations in my sanctified life that will provide opportunities for me to reaffirm the initial commitment. Making Him Lord of my life in one moment of consecration must be followed by keeping Him Lord of my life.

Continual Cleansing

As we walk in this kind of obedience, His blood cleanses us. From what? Weren't we cleansed once and for all?

We cannot receive a once-for-all cleansing and then go our merry way in self-reliance. We must rely daily on the blood of Christ for continual cleansing.

We need His blood to cleanse us from the thousands of times we unknowingly fall short of His perfect standard. We need Christ's blood to continually cleanse us of every thought, attitude, word, or deed that does not edify and encourage. We need Christ's blood to cleanse us from the daily accumulation of "dust" we gather by traveling the roads of this world.

Theologian Mildred Wynkoop illustrates this continued cleansing by asking readers to imagine themselves as suffering from defective kidneys. There is no hope in yourself—your blood supply is self-polluting. The only hope lies outside—if you can be attached periodically to a machine that will cleanse your blood. But suppose there was a way in which you could be attached to a healthy friend so that his kidneys could cleanse your polluted blood. Suppose that this friend was willing to be connected to you. So long as you were connected to this friend, and walking step by step with him, your friend would insure a continuing perfection of your blood supply. An entire life-style would be established to maintain this moment-by-moment cleansing.

This is what holiness is all about. It is being connected to Christ in a daily obedient walk of submission. It is walking where He leads. It is relying on Christ, and Him alone, for cleansing.

Holiness is Christlikeness. Christlikeness is not reserved for a select few older saints or ministers. It is for every believer. Holiness is for ordinary people.

From *Holiness for Ordinary People,* by Keith Drury. Copyright 1983 by the Wesley Press, Marion, Ind. Used by permission.

Pride:

A Scene from Life

Gary got up from the altar, forgiven of a sin he probably didn't commit. Here's what happened.

Gary works as a welder in a factory. He has always thought of himself as a good welder—in fact, one of the best in his shop.

Last month his suspicion was confirmed by one of the company's vice presidents. The pin-striped suit and shiny hard hat walked into the shop and asked the foreman to call Gary away from his fountain of sparks.

The suit spoke to the welder. "For several years now, we've been hearing compliments about you from your bosses. And we thought it was time we thanked you in a special way for your fine work." And out of the suit came a $1,000 check.

Needless to say, Gary told his coworkers. He told friends in church. And he called his parents who live across the country. He even thought about telling the clerk in the neighborhood hardware store. But he decided not to.

Then came the guilt. He read Proverbs 16:18, "Pride goes before destruction."

In his bragging, Gary now saw himself as a soaring eagle, strutting his stuff. But the scripture seemed to be saying he was nothing more than a worm on a hang glider, and that he'd better come back down to earth.

For Christian eagles and worms, Jon Johnston has some advice.

Chapter 4

How Proud Is Too Proud?

by Jon Johnston

Background Scripture: Proverbs 16:18; Romans 8:16-17; Philippians 2:3-4; 1 Peter 2:9

DO YOU SUFFER from a poor self-image? The book *How to Be a Household Word* offers some tongue-in-cheek advice. Use it and you're promised instant celebrity status—even if you lack beauty, brains, brawn, or bankroll.

Suggestions include: handcuff yourself to someone already famous; brag about the deplorable gasoline mileage your Rolls Royce is getting; invent a glow-in-the-dark *TV Guide;* have someone page you every five minutes.

If none of these help, give a quick call to the International Star Registry in Toronto. For only a few dollars they will name a star after you, and send you a sky chart to pinpoint its location.

We smile at these bizarre suggestions, yet we have probably witnessed equally amusing attempts to bolster self-esteem. People who change clothes six times a day, who play and replay "How Great I Am" cassette tapes, or who spend megadollars for cosmetic surgery—only to look worse.

Although most of us resist such extremes, we are also concerned about self-image. And concerned we should be. For a healthy, positive view of ourselves is crucial to our total well-being.

Self-esteem: More than an Accessory

Self-esteem refers to those thoughts, feelings, and attitudes we have toward ourselves. We see ourselves as more or less intelligent or as stupid, competent or klutzy, lovable or abrasive, captivating or boring.

The conclusions we draw concerning ourselves are based on the following considerations:

- appraisal of our performance;
- view of the way we think others judge us;
- evaluation of ourselves about our value or potential as a human being.

Of course, these three sources feed constant data into our psyche. And since the data varies from day to day, depending on life's situations and our moods, there are fluctuations in our sense of self-esteem. In short, the way we feel about ourselves is often affected by other people and situations that arise.

As a result, disappointment associated with such things as dismissal from work, marital conflict, and loss of valuable property can dampen feelings of self-worth. On the other hand, a big pay raise, a friendly smile, or a vacation in Hawaii can make us feel taller than a New York skyscraper.

In spite of these situations, it is imperative that we maintain a core of vibrant, positive self-esteem—especially when times get tough.

Why is self-respect so necessary? Bruce Narramore, Christian psychologist, suggests these reasons.

1. *SIGNIFICANCE.* Positive self-esteem provides us with the assurance that we count—that our lives make a difference. We are more than an "infinitesimal, noisy speck of scum floating about on a bit of matter in the universe."[1] Much more. And to know this fact provides fulfillment, meaning, and a real sense of purpose for our daily life.

2. *SELF-CONFIDENCE.* A healthy self-image is a vaccine against crippling levels of anxiety, fear, and insecurity. In place of fear, we have an undergirding trust in our abilities—and the way those abilities will help us successfully cope in the future. The "can do" attitude is essential. For with it we can more easily brush aside the temptation to feel inferior, and we can reach out to tackle new challenges.

3. *SECURITY.* While self-confidence is focused more on the *internal* ("I'll pass the exam!"), security beams in on our *external* world ("I trust my friends"). When our self-esteem is

low, the world seems fraught with danger. Like Chicken Little, we too quickly see the sky collapsing and we forecast inevitable doom. By contrast, when we have an upbeat self-image, we see the world as a better place. As a result, we feel much more relaxed, hopeful, and secure.

Point established: a healthy self-image has lots of benefits. The payoff is great in terms of mental and physical health, compatibility with others and enjoyment of life.

But just how does the experience we know as "entire sanctification" square with this needed quality of self-esteem?

Total Consecration: Gateway to Self-respect

When we are born again, or receive *initial* sanctification, *past sins* are forgiven and all things become new. The bridges of our past—those of corruption, defeat, and sin—are burned. We begin to walk on our new, lighted pathway. We follow our new, trustworthy Trailguide—the very Light of the World.

Having repented of past sins, and believed that God has forgiven those acts of disobedience, we see ourselves as pardoned, as no longer rebels to His will and righteousness. We have laid down our arms and received His loving forgiveness.

The result is immediate. It does wonders for our self-image when we see ourselves as no longer warring against the Ruler of the universe. No longer are we dogged by pangs of guilt. Now we are aligned on the side of right. Enter: deep, inner peace, and an abiding sense of freedom and hope.

But this is only the beginning. God wants to do more for our self-image than relieve it of guilt.

In His mercy, He has made provision for a glorious second work of grace—commonly referred to as "entire sanctification." In receiving this grace, our sinful nature is instantaneously cleansed. Our original *sin* (in contrast to the *acts* of sin that are forgiven in initial sanctification), which we inherited from Adam, is completely removed.

When such a catastrophic event takes place in our lives, the results are: (1) *PURITY OF HEART* (see Acts 15:8-9) and (2) *POWER TO WITNESS* (see Acts 1:8). In short, there is a complete transformation (see Romans 12:1-2).[2]

And what effect does this have on our self-esteem? The kind of complete consecration involved in entire sanctification causes us to see ourselves as *cleansed and empowered children of God*.

As His children, we know that we're in harmony with His master plan for our lives. He is the Vine, of which we are fruit-bearing branches. What fruit do we bear? The fruit of the Spirit: love, joy, peace, patience, kindness, goodness, faithfulness, gentleness, and self-control. In short, the embodiment of the holy life.

To be assured of our inward holiness does far more for our self-image than anything such as riches, praise, or lofty position. What could compare with being a child of the King. 1 Peter 2:9 says it all.

> You are a chosen people, a royal priesthood, a holy nation, a people belonging to God, that you may declare the praises of him who called you out of darkness into his wonderful light.

Does entire sanctification really change our self-image? Let me tell you a short story.

A dear friend of mine was in her early 60s, but her black hair and wrinkleless smile made her look many years younger. Her spirit was jubilant. Her life was dedicated to helping others—especially those who others shunned. As a result, she felt good about herself.

Then it all hit in staccato rhythm. The agonizing pain, the endless wait in doctors' offices, the prognosis—and finally, the exploratory surgery.

My wife, Cherry, and I stood beside her husband in the waiting room. The grim-faced surgeon entered with the depressing news: "I couldn't get all the cancer. It's just a matter of time." Our hearts sank and tears welled up in our eyes.

Then came the trip home, and the long days ahead—three years worth. She knew of her plight, and that knowledge changed her completely. The smile was replaced by a frown. The joyous spirit gave way to one of deep depression. Kindness toward others departed from her life. Instead she seemed to want others to share her grief and pain. So she blamed, complained, lashed out. Soon her wish was granted. We suffered too.

During this time I began reading books that deepened my understanding of entire sanctification. Writers like John Wesley, J. Kenneth Grider, and Oswald Chambers helped me understand the transforming effects of this glorious experience on the attitudes of people. In particular, I realized that total consecration reforms and revitalizes self-concept.

But what about my friend? Could her anguishing spirit be helped? Could she find a deep settled peace in the midst of unbearable pain and discouragement? Absolutely! God's Word makes no exceptions!

Cherry and I began to pray fervently. We met with our pastor to share our commitment, and to request his help—for we knew that our friend had confidence in his life.

Soon thereafter we went with our minister to visit her. Immediately she went into her customary tirade. We listened as she revealed the deep hurt. At last she became quiet.

Our minister moved close to her pillow, offered words of comfort, and asked if she would like him to pray. She nodded yes. Before praying he told her to be completely open to whatever God had to say. She nodded again.

Then came the prayer that made the difference. It was a prayer that explained the necessity of coming to God for a second work of grace. A grace that would purify the heart and provide a reservoir of spiritual power. A grace that would destroy Satan's reign in the spirit. A grace that would bring complete victory through total surrender.

My friend listened to each word. Her lips began to move as she joined in. It wasn't long before tears began to stream down those thin cheeks. Then came the wonderful climax when she raised her boney arms to heaven in submission. The floodgates of heaven opened as she began praising God for purifying her life. For taking away all bitterness, all resentment, all self-pity.

After the prayer, she looked up. The beautiful smile had returned. Even the tone of her voice was softer as she witnessed to the new work of grace that had taken place in her heart. We listened and rejoiced. Then we left.

That isn't the end of the story. There were more days of

severe tribulation ahead. The pain grew worse. Even the strongest drugs didn't seem to help.

But my sister in Christ saw it all in a different light. Her spirit said, "Yes Lord. I am ready for whatever You want of me." She asked certain people for forgiveness. She witnessed to others. People who visited would say, "I came here depressed, but left hopeful and encouraged."

Go ahead. Theologize about the doctrine of entire sanctification. We need to understand its scriptural basis. That helps us all. But in your lofty and complex explanations, remember that the ultimate value of the second work of grace lies in its positive effect on the lives of people—like my friend—who "was blind but began to see," who was in the pit of hopelessness but rose to the mountain peak of glory.

Looking for a self-esteem that yields abundant significance, self-confidence, and security? Draw freely from this bottomless well. Allow His Spirit to bear witness with your spirit that you are a child of God!

When Self-esteem Goes to Seed

Just as certainly as healthy self-esteem brings rich fulfillment to our lives, self-worship invariably yields disaster.

The Book of Proverbs minces no words when it warns us against an obsessive arrogance of spirit:

When pride comes, then comes *disgrace,* but with humility comes wisdom *(11:2).*

Pride goes before *destruction,* a haughty spirit before a *fall (16:18).*

A man's pride brings him *low,* but a man of lowly spirit gains honor *(29:23).*

However, the book's most stinging rebuke of pride is in listing it *first* among the things God hates:

There are six things the Lord hates, seven that are detestable to him: *haughty eyes,* a lying tongue . . . *(6:17).*

Theologian Reinhold Niebuhr states that, in comparing the damaging effects of despair and of an overrated optimism about self, the latter wreaks far more havoc on the Christian. No doubt about it, the way to spell spiritual defeat is P-R-I-D-E.

With this in mind, we ask: What are the differences between authentic self-esteem that is generated from a pure heart, and sinful pride?

First, unlike pride, biblical self-esteem is compatible with true humility. Sanctified self-esteem is totally consistent with the poverty of spirit that Jesus admonished His followers to possess.

In sharp contrast to the vain person, one with biblical self-esteem knows that his worth is based on the Master Potter's craftsmanship. His life, like clay, has been molded into something beautiful by a loving God.

Nevertheless, he never ceases to recall the depths of his prior existence. As Isaiah vividly states: He remembers "the hole of the pit [from] whence [his clay was] digged" (Isaiah 51:1, KJV). As a result, he possesses an abiding humility.

The proud person, by contrast, boasts of his own powers. To hear him tell it, he's self-made—and he worships his "maker."

Second, unlike pride, biblical self-esteem does not manifest a defensive spirit. It operates on a simple motto: nothing to prove, nothing to lose.

A fully consecrated heart provides the kind of inner assurance that welcomes accountability: nothing to hide, an open-book life. Willing to face the truth. Willing to accept and deal honestly with legitimate criticism.

Not so with the arrogant person. Unwilling to be transparent and vulnerable, he hides, denies, runs, lies. When that ceases to work, and he is forced to be accountable, he starts to build walls. Nothing is admitted. As a result, nothing is corrected. He remains as static as he remains unbending.

Excuses are manufactured for every weakness:
I'm not dogmatic, just "sure of myself."
I'm not judging, only "discerning."
I'm not argumentative, just "trying to prove a point."
And I'm certainly not stubborn, I'm "confident in my position."

43

Who could ever penetrate such impregnable barriers? Who could ever get through to such a solid defense?

Third, in contrast to pride, holiness-generated self-esteem *focuses on serving others.*

The self-serving spirit of our age is evident in the words of well-known commercials:

"Have it your way."

"Do yourself a favor."

"You deserve a break today."

Not so with the humble, but self-respecting, Spirit-filled believer. He takes to heart the words of Philippians 2:3-4:

> Do nothing out of selfish ambition or vain conceit, but *in humility consider others better than yourselves.* Each of you should look not only to your own interests, but also to the interests of others *(italics added).*

Tuned to his selfish wavelength, the arrogant person broadcasts and manipulates his way through life. Agreeing with former football coach Vince Lombardi, he declares with clenched fist: "Winning is everything!" He insists on supremacy, even in seemingly unimportant areas. So much to prove to so many people—especially himself.

The mere thought of condescending to help another in need is out of the question. Servanthood is for the weak-spirited. The softies. Unless, of course, there is something big to gain in the way of publicity or leverage.

Losers and Finders

Old-timers offered this advice to anyone wanting to live the life of holiness: *Die out to self.* In short, renounce your "right" to go your own way.

Jesus stated it another way:

> If anyone would come after me, he must *deny* himself and take up his cross and follow me. For whoever . . . loses his life for me and for the gospel will save it *(Mark 8:34-35).*

It sounds contradictory. Die to gain life—just like a kernel of wheat does. Losing life to save it.

Real living begins when we nail carnal self to the Cross. In doing so, these "brothers" must die:

- *SELF-JUSTIFICATION:* unwillingness to accept God's reproofs and correction;
- *SELF-INDULGENCE:* laziness, sensuality without discipline;
- *SELF-EXALTATION:* inability to resign to God's will;
- *SELF-EXONERATION:* belief in own rightness and righteousness.[3]

When does this ugly family die, so we can be all God wants us to be? God's Word is very emphatic. It is when we totally consecrate ourselves to Him. When we place the most stubbornly disobedient aspect of our personality, our will, on the altar—and proclaim Him, alone, to be our sovereign Lord.

Respected author Sam Shoemaker offers a clear, ringing testimony to entire sanctification's affect on himself. His words encapsulate, and his life incarnates, the truths expressed in this chapter.

> I can well remember a time in my life, long after my first decisive spiritual experience, when I was facing the need to take another big step forward. I could almost see myself shrinking out of sight under the withering effects of an honest facing of my faults.
>
> When I let go deeply inside, my true "self" was never more fulfilled and expressed, and I realized that all this fanfare of resistance and self-will is the protective device of the ego to keep the true "self" from emerging and being victorious.
>
> This fear of giving up, or giving in, is a contrivance of the ego. As Fenelon said, "If we looked carefully into ourselves, we should find some secret place where we hide what we think we are not obliged to sacrifice to God." But *until that false ego dies, the true self cannot live.* And the death of an ego is the greatest of all human crises.[4]

---

1. E. S. Mann, *The Things That Count: Twelve Challenges to Dynamic Living* (Kansas City: Beacon Hill Press of Kansas City, 1983), 139.

2. The word Paul uses for being "transformed" from the world is *metamorphousthai,* from which we obtain our word "metamorphosis." Implied is a transformation of the very essence of inward being (e.g., cocoon into butterfly).

3. Merne A. Harris, "The Carnal Nature," Comp. Kenneth Geiger, in *Insights into Holiness* (Kansas City: Beacon Hill Press, 1963), 45.

4. Sam Shoemaker, *How You Can Find Happiness* (New York: E. P. Dutton & Company, Inc.). Quoted by John E. Riley, "Holiness—Crisis and Process," in *Insights into Holiness* (Kansas City: Beacon Hill Press, 1963), 94.

Temperament:

A Scene from Life

John is a sanctified bulldozer, so he says.

But if you want to confirm his sanctification, don't ask his secretary.

"You make one small mistake and he goes up like a flare," she says. "He's pushy, domineering, and insensitive. And when he doesn't get his way, he explodes. I'll tell you, I've peeled him off the wall more than once."

John explains that aggressiveness is just his nature. "I was born with it, and I'll die with it." Sanctification, he says, doesn't touch it because the two don't play in the same ballpark.

I don't want to shock you, but there's a good possibility John is, in fact, a sanctified bulldozer.

Sanctification does not pop a person's temperament inside out faster than the speed of glory. It does do some serious chiseling off of the rough spots, but as far as your basic temperament is concerned, you're probably stuck with the one you've got. That's the bad news.

The good news is Keith Drury will tell you how to make the most of what you've got.

Chapter 5

Will Holiness Change My Temperament?

by Keith Drury

Background Scripture: Acts 8:1-2; 9:1-2; 26:1, 19b-25

DOES ENTIRE SANCTIFICATION give us a new temperament? Will it make a boisterous extrovert into a calm and quiet individual? Or are we "stuck" with our individual temperaments with little hope of changing in this life? These are questions we will examine here.

What Is Temperament?

Temperament is not character. Character refers to traits developed through personal discipline, training, and God's grace. Honesty, loyalty, kindness, and patience are character traits. No person may say he or she is born with a natural tendency to these traits of character.

Temperament, on the other hand, is a natural inclination. We are born with it. Our temperaments are set in our genes and honed by our environment and childhood. Temperament is what makes some of us outgoing or extroverted, and others quiet, shy, and introverted. Temperament is what makes one child bold and aggressive while his sister or brother is shy and dependent.

One analysis of temperament types deals with four basic temperament categories. We will use four individuals to illustrate these basic types of temperaments. Please meet JoAnne, John, Sharon, and Jim.

JoAnne. When JoAnne enters a room of people, she seems to "fill it up" with her personality. She is talkative, personable, and outgoing. She loves people and seldom meets anyone she considers a stranger. She flits from one small group to another, chattering with each person as if that person is her very best friend. She easily gathers people around her and rallies them to a task—she is frequently called on to be a leader of something new. Where there's action, you'll find JoAnne at the center of it.

John. Few people are as forceful as John. He seems to wind up as the leader of every group he gets involved with. John is a hard driver, likes to get things done, a builder. He has no trouble making decisions—even for other people. Most folk recognize that his natural abilities equip him to be the boss of just about anything. He likes to take new things and is always launching some new project at home, at work, or in his local church. John is respected—even feared—by most people.

Sharon. Sharon works with fifth graders all week, then spends most of the weekend working with children in her local church. She is calm, easygoing, and well liked by just about everyone. She is systematic and so well organized that others marvel at the quantity of work she gets done with so little fuss. Though she does not get involved with everything, she will carry through on any commitment she makes. Her loyalty is deep.

Jim. Jim is the opposite of JoAnne. He doesn't prefer to be in large groups; and when he is forced into one, he would rather sit to the side and keep quiet. He is extremely creative, artistic, and is a deeper thinker than any of his associates. He is always thinking of a better way to do things. He blossoms into a chattering speech when someone talks about philosophy and theory. Jim is extremely sensitive. People sometimes hurt him without even knowing it. When he is "up," he can produce more ideas in a few minutes about how to do something than most people can in several hours. He is definitely the most creative person in his group.

These four—JoAnne, John, Sharon, and Jim—represent the four basic temperament types. Jim is a writer and part-time artist; Sharon is a schoolteacher; John is a boss; and JoAnne is a district sales manager for a home sales company. Using the oldest categories of temperament types, JoAnne would be a "sanguine," John a "choleric," Sharon a "phlegmatic," and Jim a "melancholic."

Each of us usually leans toward one of these basic types of temperament. Of course, none of us are 100% of any one temperament. Generally, we have a dominant temperament type, a secondary type, while the other two remain recessive. Such temperament traits are a result of our inherited characteristics and environment shaping. Each of us is different and has his own particular strengths and weaknesses.

The Dark Side of Temperaments

So far we have only spoken about the strengths of these four temperament types. On the other side there are corresponding weaknesses or "besetting sins" for each temperament type. JoAnne, John, Sharon, and Jim are all members of a "covenant cell group." One week they were studying the idea of besetting sins, and each requested prayer support for the areas where they are tempted most. What were these requests?

JoAnne, the outgoing sales manager, confessed she was undisciplined in her devotions, not submissive to authority, and feared that she was often too egocentric.

John, the boss, confessed a serious problem at home with anger, a tendency to be proud, and that he often was dominating, pushy, and insensitive with his employees at work.

Sharon, the teacher, asked for prayer relative to her inclination to be stingy, her fearfulness of launching out to do new things for the Lord, and her extreme defensiveness whenever anyone offered her suggestions or advice—especially her husband.

Jim, the writer-artist, expressed concern for his tendency to be criticial of others—always thinking of how they "ought to" do things, for his moody behavior at home, and his negative attitudes of doubt.

Holiness and Temperament

Now, what does all this have to do with holiness and entire sanctification? Does sanctification change our temperaments? Will JoAnne become quiet and submissive when she is sanctified? Will God make John easygoing like Sharon? Will sanctification make Sharon aggressive and generous? Will the Holy Spirit even out Jim's moods? What relationship does entire sanctification have to temperaments?

1. Entire sanctification does not destroy our natural tem-

peraments. Extroverts do not become introverts. Pessimists do not become optimists. Aggressive, high-powered people do not become passive and shy. Sanctification results in a refinement and a purification of our natural temperaments. In sanctification, God harnesses and redirects our strengths. He provides new power over our besetting sins. God needs an infinite variety of personality qualities to do His work. He is not in the business of making cookie-cutter believers.

2. *God's cleansing will bring a new power over besetting sin.* This is one of the reasons people differ so widely as to what God actually does through entire sanctification. JoAnne may claim God gave her new self-discipline and a spirit of submission. John realizes a fresh love and sensitivity for his employees. Sharon experiences a new motivation to get involved. And Jim has a newfound power over his critical spirit. Each has experiences the same work of God. Yet, the area of cleansing is different and quite related to his or her temperament traits. Whatever our besetting sin, God wants to cleanse our hearts of the inclination to it. He does this through entire sanctification.

3. *As we grow in the sanctified life, God continues to mold our personality strengths.* He will help JoAnne harness her extrovertism to make her a better witness for the gospel. He will gradually channel John's energy into leading other believers to accomplish His work. He progressively strengthens Sharon's loyalty so that she becomes the "right-hand woman" of the church. He will keep developing Jim's creativity so that it is directed into practical and helpful work, and not mere theory. All this is accomplished as a sanctified person daily submits to the Lordship of Christ. Heart purity may be the work of an instant. But continual growth in Christian personality is a lifetime work.

4. *Not only does the Lord develop the strengths of our own temperament, He also brings us strengths not inherent to our own basic personality.* This too is an ever-expanding work of the Holy Spirit. As we submit daily to His work and leadings, He begins to bring strengths to us that are largely foreign to our natural temperament. For instance, as JoAnne is totally obedient to the Lord, she may become a leading example of self-discipline and submission—even though her basic temperament

does not include her to be so. A bossy John may become exceptionally sensitive and loving toward other people. A defensive Sharon may become extremely open and vulnerable. And an unsociable Jim may become quite friendly to a neighbor he wants to win to Christ.

So while the initial work of sanctification immediately impacts us regarding our besetting sins, God works progressively at developing our strengths throughout our entire lives. This expanding work will bring personality strengths to us that are not even inherent in our natural temperament.

5. Perfect Christlikeness is found in the Body of Christ. Evangelist Jimmy Johnson is adept at making this truth clear. His idea: (A) Christ was the perfect personality—He exhibited all the strengths of all four temperament types. (B) None of us will ever arrive at this absolute perfection of personality on earth. (C) Unbelievers must somehow, somewhere, see this perfect Christlikeness. (D) Perfect Christlikeness is found in the Church—the Body of Christ.

As we gather together as a Body, each with our own unique strengths, Christ is seen. And, just as examining a finger or an ear does not give us a total picture of a human body, so examining one individual believer will not give a total picture of what Jesus is like. Yet, the corporate body of believers illustrates pure Christlikeness—one believer illustrates one strength and another believer exemplifies a different strength.

This "corporate holiness" does not get us off the hook relative to personal holiness. On the contrary, our motivation to become Christlike is greater as we recognize that we are part of a grand body of believers who together do, in fact, illustrate all the strengths of Jesus Christ. In this sense we are truly part of the Body of Christ.

Thus, any search for a perfect example of holiness will lead the seeker to both the Word of God and to the Body of Christ. In the Word of God we see Jesus the perfect example. When the Body of Christ is taken as a total group, we catch a glimpse of the same traits of Jesus Christ.

From *Holiness for Ordinary People,* by Keith Drury. Copyright 1983 by the Wesley Press, Marion, Ind. Used by permission.

Anger:
A Scene from Life

Bobby Lee Sanders is an accountant who can't tell a pipe wrench from a crowbar. That's why his wife didn't want him to try to fix the leak in the faucet outside the house.

But it was a small leak.

In less than two minutes he had broken off the copper pipe about two feet inside the house. And since he didn't think to turn off the water first, he created an early afternoon shower in the downstairs family room.

Now when Bobby Lee's wife saw all that water surge through the ceiling and onto the TV, her personality went into a spasm.

Though she stopped short of swearing, she proceeded to call her husband nearly everything but a good plumber.

Did Bobby Lee's wife behave like the sanctified Christian she professes to be? Or should she have patted him on the head and said, "Well, you tried Snookems," and then smiled as she dialed the plumber?

Or should the lady have simply stared a glare and left it there.

The answer is not obvious, you know. Let's read what James Dobson has to say about anger in the Christian life.

Chapter 6

Do Saints Get Angry?

by James Dobson

Background Scripture: Romans 12:14-19; Ephesians 4:26-27;
  James 1:19-20

I DECIDED TO SURPRISE MY WIFE with a corsage on Easter Sunday morning, being a firm believer in marital "flower power." The local florist took my order and promised that an orchid would be ready after five o'clock Saturday night. All week long I harbored this noble deed in my generous heart, smiling to myself and anticipating the moment of truth after breakfast the following Sunday.

When Saturday afternoon rolled around, I found a phony excuse to leave in the car for a few minutes, and drove to the florist to retrieve the secret package. The shop was crowded with customers and the lady behind the counter was obviously overworked and stressed. My first mistake, I suppose, was in not perceiving her tension soon enough, or the beads of sweat that ringed her upper lip. I patiently waited my turn and watched each patron carry his order past me and out the door. When I finally reached the counter and gave my name, the saleslady shuffled through a stack of tickets, and then said matter-of-factly, "We're not going to be able to fill your order. You'll just have to get your flowers somewhere else."

She did not offer a reason or apologize for the error. Her voice had a definite take-it-or-leave-it sound, which I found irritating. She stood, hands on hips, glaring at me as though *I* had somehow caused the mistake.

At first I was puzzled, and then I asked, "Why did you accept my order if you were unable to prepare it? I could have gone somewhere else, but now it is too late to buy a corsage at another shop."

I remember distinctly that my response was very controlled under the circumstances, although my displeasure was no doubt apparent. My brief question had no sooner been uttered when a curtain swung open at the rear of the building and a red-faced man burst into the shop. He stormed toward me and pressed his chest against mine. I had no idea how big he was; I only know that I'm six-foot-two and weigh 190 pounds, yet, my eyes focused somewhere between his pulsating Adam's apple and his quivering chin. It was immediately apparent that Goliath was not merely upset—he was livid with rage! He curled his lip upward and shook his clenched fist in the vicinity of my jaw.

For the next two minutes or so, he unloaded the most violent verbal attack I had ever sustained. He used every curse word I knew and then taught me a few I hadn't even heard in the Army. Then after questioning my heritage, he announced his intention of throwing a certain portion of my anatomy out the front door.

It is difficult to describe the emotional shock of that moment. It was a conflict I neither sought nor anticipated. Suddenly, without warning, I had tripped a spring that must have been winding tighter and tighter throughout the hectic day (or year). The next move was clearly mine. Silence fell on the shop as a half-dozen customers gasped and awaited my response.

The toughest part of the encounter involved the instantaneous conflict between what my impulses dictated and what God had been trying to teach me. In a matter of two or three seconds, it seemed as though the Lord said to me, "Are you going to obey Me, or not?" I muttered some kind of defensive reply, and then did the most difficult thing I had ever been required to do: I turned on my heels and walked from the shop. To the customers, I probably appeared cowardly—especially in view of the size of my adversary. Or, perhaps they assumed I could think of no appropriate reply. All of these agitating thoughts reverberated through my head as I walked to my car.

Did I go home in triumph at having done what God wanted of me? Certainly not immediately. Hot blood pulsed through my neck and ears, and adrenaline surged through my veins. My immediate response was to do something primitive—like heave a brick through the window where a bouquet of roses sat. Gradually, however, my physiological state returned to normal and I looked back on my restraint with some satisfaction.

The kind of frustration I experienced in the floral shop, whether it be called anger or some related emotion, is of importance to others trying to live the Christian life. I'm not the only one who has had to learn how to control his tongue and the tumultuous undercurrents that often propel it. But what *does* God expect of us in this area of our lives? Does He want us to be bland, colorless individuals who have no feelings at all? Is all anger sinful? There are many related questions with theological implications that we will consider in the discussion that follows.

What Is Anger? When Is It Sinful?

Let's begin with the question, Is all anger sinful?

Obviously, not everything that can be identified under the heading of anger is violation of God's law, for Ephesians 4:26 instructs us to "be angry but do not sin" (RSV). That verse says to me that there is a difference between *strong feelings,* and the seething hostility that is consistently condemned in the Scripture. Our first task, it would appear, is to clarify that distinction.

Well, how about the emotion you experienced in the floral shop? You were no doubt angry when you walked toward the door. Was God displeased by what you were feeling?

I don't think so, and I felt no condemnation afterward. It's important to remember that anger is not only emotional—it is biochemical as well. The unprovoked assault by the store owner was perceived by me as enormously threatening. It didn't take an extended analysis to figure that out! In such a situation, the human body is equipped with an automatic defensive system, called the "flight or fight" mechanism, which prepares the entire organism for action. Adrenaline is pumped into the bloodstream, which sets off a series of physiological responses within the body. Blood pressure is increased in accordance with an acceleration in heartbeat; the eyes are dilated for better peripheral vision; the hands get sweaty and the mouth gets dry; and the muscles are supplied with a sudden burst of energy. In a matter of seconds, the individual is transformed from a quiet condition to an "alarm reaction state." *Most importantly, this is an involuntary response that occurs whether or not we will it.*

Once the flight or fight hormones are released, it is impossible to ignore the intense feelings they precipitate. It would be like denying the existence of a toothache or any other tumultuous physical occurrence. And since God created this system as a means by which the body can protect itself against danger, I do not believe He condemns us for its proper functioning.

On the other hand, our *reaction* to the feeling of anger is more deliberate and responsive to voluntary control. When we sullenly replay the agitating event over and over in our minds, grinding our teeth in hostility and seeking opportunities for revenge, or lash out in some overt act of violence, then it is logical to assume that we cross over the line into sinfulness. If this interpretation of the scripture is accurate, then the exercise of the *will* stands in the gap between the two halves of the verse "be angry . . . do not sin."

How would you define the emotion of anger?

Anger is a complicated response that has become a sort of catchall phrase. Many of the behaviors that have been included under the heading of anger may have nothing to do with sinful behavior. Consider these examples:

Extreme frustration gives rise to an emotional response that we also call anger. I have seen this reaction from a high school basketball player, for example, who had an off night where everything went wrong. Perhaps he fumbled the ball away and double dribbled and missed all his shots at the basket. The more he tried, the worse he played, and the more foolish he felt. Such frustration can trigger a volcanic emotional discharge at the coach or anyone in his way. Such are the irritations that cause golf clubs to be wrapped around trees and tennis rackets to be impaled on net posts.

Rejection is another occurrence that often generates a kind of angry response. A girl who is jilted by the boy she loves, for example may retaliate with a flurry of harsh words. Far from hating him, however, her response is motivated by the deep hurt associated with being thrown over—discarded —disrespected.

You see, anger has come to represent many strong, negative feelings in a human being. Accordingly, I doubt if all the Scriptures that address themselves to the subject of anger are referring equally to the entire range of emotions under that broad category.

Then how do the apparently innocent emotions you have described differ from sinful anger?

Your question raises a theological issue that may be difficult to communicate, yet it is of utmost importance to Christians everywhere. The Bible teaches the existence of a potentially disastrous flaw in the character of man that urges him toward sinful behavior, even though he may desire to serve God. Paul referred to this inner struggle in Romans 7:21-24: "So I find this law at work: When I want to do good, evil is right there with me. For in my inner being I delight in God's law; but I see another law at work in the members of my body, waging war against the law of my mind and making me a prisoner of the law of sin at work within my members. What a wretched man I am! Who will rescue me from this body of death?"

You see, Paul was speaking as a Christian, yet he admitted the existence of an internal war between good and evil. Anger, jealousy, envy, etc., are products of this inner nature. Paul was not unique in that regard, for the same predisposition has been inherited by the entire human race. David confessed, "In sin did my mother conceive me" (Psalm 51:5, RSV). It is, in effect, the "sin living in me" (Romans 7:17) as opposed to sins that I commit.

Now, what does this have to do with the subject of anger? Simply this: our inbred sinful nature gives rise to a response that we might call "carnal anger," which must be distinguished from anger as a function of frustration or the endocrine system, or emotional and psychological needs. It is, instead, contrary to everything holy and righteous, *and cannot by any human striving be nullified.*

Virtually every orthodox denomination acknowledges the biblical teaching I have described, for it is hardly escapable in the Scriptures. However, great disagreement occurs between Christians in regard to the *resolution* of the problem. The difference in teaching lies in whether or not it *can* be cleansed in this life and under what circumstances. It is my belief that the Holy Spirit, through an act of divine grace, cleanses and purifies the heart (see Acts 15:8-9) in order "that the body of sin might be done away with" (Romans 6:6).

What are the characteristics of carnal anger?
What aspects of it does God condemn in the Bible?

I see unacceptable anger as that which motivates us to hurt our fellowman—when we want to slash and cut and inflict pain on another person. Remember the experience of the apostle Peter when Jesus was being crucified. His emotions were obviously in a state of turmoil, seeing his beloved Master being subjected to an unthinkable horror. However, Jesus rebuked him when he severed the high priest's servant's ear with a sword. If there ever was a person with an excuse to lash out in anger, Peter seemed to be justified; nevertheless Jesus did not accept his behavior, and He compassionately healed the wounded man.

There is a vitally important message for all of us in this recorded event. *Nothing* justifies an attitude of hatred or a desire to harm another person, and we are treading on dangerous ground when our thoughts and actions begin leading us in that direction. Not even the defense of Jesus Christ would justify that kind of aggression.

Are you saying that being "right" on an issue does not purify a wrong attitude or behavior?

Yes. In fact, having been in the church all my life, I've observed that Christians are often in greater danger when they are "right" in conflict than when they are clearly wrong. In other words, a person is more likely to become bitter and deeply hostile when someone has cheated him or taken advantage of him than is the offender himself. E. Stanley Jones agreed, stating that a Christian is more likely to sin by his reactions than his actions.

If anger is unquestionably sinful when it leads us to hurt another person, then is the evil only involved in the aggressive act itself? What if we become greatly hostile but hold it inside where it is never revealed?

John told us that hatred for a brother is equivalent to

murder (see 1 John 3:15). Thus, sinful anger can occur in the mind, even if it is never translated into overt behavior.

How Do You Deal with Anger?

Many psychologists seem to feel that all anger should be ventilated or verbalized. They say it is emotionally and physically harmful to repress or withhold any intense feeling. Can you harmonize this scientific understanding with the scriptural commandment that "everyone should be quick to listen, slow to speak and slow to become angry" (James 1:19).

Personally, I do not find these objectives to be in contradiction. God does not want us to repress our anger—sending it unresolved into the memory bank. Why else did the apostle Paul tell us to settle our irritations before sundown each day (see Ephesians 4:26), effectively preventing accumulation of seething hostility with the passage of time?

But how can intense negative feelings be resolved or ventilated without blasting away at the offender—an act that is specifically prohibited by the Scripture? Are there other ways of releasing pent-up emotions? Yes, including the following:

- by making the irritation a matter of prayer;
- by explaining our negative feelings to a mature and understanding third party who can advise and lead;
- by going to an offender and showing a spirit of love and forgiveness;
- by understanding that God often permits most frustrating and agitating events to occur so as to teach us patience and help us grow;
- by realizing that *no* offense by another person could possibly equal our guilt before God, yet He has for-

given us; are we not obligated to show the same mercy to others?

These are just a few of the mechanisms and attitudes that act to neutralize a spirit of resentment.

I have a great deal of resentment and anger toward my father, for what he did to me and my mother when I was a child. I have struggled with these deep feelings for years; I don't want to hurt him, but I can't forget the pain he caused me and the rest of our family. How can I come to terms with the problem?

After laying the matter before God and asking for His healing touch, I would suggest that you examine the *perspective* in which you see your dad. I attempted to explain this point in my book *What Wives Wish Their Husbands Knew About Women,* and believe it will be helpful at this point:

A very close and respected friend of mine, whom I'll call Martha, has a father who has never revealed any depth of love for her. Though she is now grown and has two children of her own, she continues to hope that he will suddenly become what he has never been. This experience causes Martha repeated disappointment and frustration. When her infant son failed to survive his first week of life, her insensitive father didn't even come to the funeral. He still shows little interest in Martha or her family—a fact that has caused deep wounds and scars through the years.

After receiving a letter from Martha in which she again mentioned her father's latest insult (he refused to come to her son's wedding), I sent her a few reactions and suggestions.

"Martha, I am more convinced every day that a great portion of our adult effort is invested in the quest for that which was *unreachable* in childhood. The more painful the early void, the more we are motivated to fill it later in life. Your dad never met the needs that a father should satisfy in his little girl, and I think you are still hoping he will miraculously become what he has never been. Therefore, he constantly disappoints you—hurts you—rejects you. I think you will be less vulnerable to pain when you accept the fact that he cannot, nor will he ever, provide the love and empathy and interest that he should. It is not easy to insulate yourself in this way. I'm still working to plug a few vacuums from my own tender years. *But it hurts less to expect nothing than to hope in vain.*

"I would guess that your dad's own childhood experiences account for his emotional peculiarities, and can perhaps be viewed as his own unique handicap. If he were blind, you would love him despite his lack of vision. In a sense, he is emotionally 'blind'. His handicap makes it *impossible* for him to perceive your feelings and anticipation. If you can accept your father as a man with a permanent handicap—one that was probably caused when *he* was vulnerable—you will shield yourself from the pick of rejection."

This letter was of help to Martha, but not because it improved her distressing circumstances. Her father is no more thoughtful and demonstrative today than he was in years past. It is Martha's *perspective* of him that has been changed.

I have a very unhappy and miserable neighbor who can't get along with anybody. She has fought with everyone she knows at one time or another. I decided that I was going to make friends with her if it was humanly possible, so I went out of my way to be kind and compassionate. I thought I had made progress toward this goal until she knocked on the front door one day and attacked me verbally. She had misunderstood something I said to another neighbor, and she came to my house to "tell me off." This woman said all the mean things she could think of, including some very insulting comments about my children, husband, and our home.

I was agitated by her attempt to hurt me when I had tried to treat her kindly, and I reacted with

irritation. We stood arguing with each other at the front door and then she left in a huff. I feel bad about the conflict now, but I don't know if I could handle it better today. What should have been my reaction?

Perhaps you realize that you missed the greatest opportunity you will probably ever have to accomplish your original objective of winning her friendship. It is difficult to convince someone of your love and respect during a period of shallow amicability. By contrast, your response to a vicious assault can instantly reveal the Christian values by which you live.

What if you had said, for example, "Mary, I don't know what you heard about me, but I think there's been a misunderstanding of what I said. Why don't you come in and we'll talk about it over a cup of coffee." Everything that you had attempted to accomplish through the previous months might have been achieved on that morning. I admit that it takes great courage and maturity to return kindness for hostility, but we are commanded by Jesus to do just that. He said in Matthew 5:43-44: "You have heard that it was said, 'Love your neighbor and hate your enemy.' But I tell you: Love your enemies and pray for those who persecute you."

I wish that I had been mature enough to have shown this Spirit of Christ to the angry man in the floral shop. As I look back on the incident, I can understand much more clearly what caused its occurrence. There are three or four holidays during the year that are most difficult for a florist, and Easter is one of them. This poor man was probably exhausted from overwork and too little sleep. The hour that I arrived (5 P.M., Saturday) represented the point of greatest fatigue, but also maximum demands from the customers. I don't excuse his offensive behavior, but it had a definite *cause*, which I should have comprehended.

I see him now, from the perspective of 10 years hence, as a hardworking fellow who was trying to earn a living and support his family. Jesus loves that man, and I must do the same. How I wish I had revealed the love of my Heavenly Father in that moment of supreme *opportunity!*

What do you have to say to the many people who sincerely try to control their anger, but who get irritated and frustrated and still lose their temper time and time again? How can they bring this area under control? Or is it impossible?

God dealt with me about my attitudes over a period of several years. He gave me gentle but firm leadership during that time, chastising me when I had failed and speaking to me through the things I read, heard, and experienced. But finally, there in the floral shop it all came to a head. It seemed in that moment of conflict the Lord asked, "Are you going to obey Me or not?"

It has been my observation that the Lord often leads us in a patient and progressively insistent manner. It begins with a mild sense of condemnation in the area where God wants us to grow and improve. Then as time goes by, a failure to respond is followed by a sense of guilt and awareness of divine disapproval. This stage leads to a period of intense awareness of God's requirements. We hear His message revealed (perhaps unwittingly) by the pastor on Sunday morning and in the books we read and even in secular programs we hear on radio and television. It seems as though the whole world is organized to convey the same decree from the Lord. And finally, we come to a crisis point where God says, "You understand what I want. *Now do it!*"

Growth in the Christian life depends on obedience in those times of crisis. The believer who refuses to accept the new obligation despite unmistakable commandments from God is destined to deteriorate spiritually. From that moment forward he begins to drift away from his Master. But for the Christian who accepts the challenge, regardless of how difficult it may be, his growth and enlightenment are assured.

John Henry Jowett said, "The will of God will never lead you where the grace of God cannot keep you." This means that the Lord won't demand something of you that He doesn't intend to help you implement.

I hope this reply will be of encouragement to those who are facing struggles in this and related matters of self-control. The Christian experience is not an easy way of life—in no instance does the Bible teach that it is. Considerable discipline is required to love our enemies and maintain a consistent prayer life and exercise sexual control and give of our income to the work of the Lord—to name but a few of the many important areas of Christian responsibility. God doesn't expect instant maturity in each of these matters, but He does require consistent growth and improvement. The beautiful part is that we are not abandoned to struggle in solitude; the Holy Spirit pities us as a father pities his child (see Psalm 103:13), tenderly leading and guiding us in the paths of righteousness.

From *Emotions: Can You Trust Them?* by James Dobson. Copyright 1980, Regal Books, Ventura, CA 93006. Used by permission.

Confrontation:
A Scene from Life

Karen is a Christian young adult who moved into an apartment she couldn't afford. So she decided to find a roommate.

Sally was the pick of the prospects—same age, Christian, likable.

Karen is not quite finicky Felix of "Odd Couple" fame, but almost. And Sally is not quite Oscar the slob, but pretty close.

Sally has the effect of a glacier. You see, she creates little mountain ranges in the apartment: a pile of shoes here, a stack of make-up there; a scattering of popcorn here, and a plate of leftovers there.

Silently, Karen dubs each minimountain a "Sally pile." And quietly she walks around the apartment, picking up the messes.

For two months now, Karen has been moving mountains. And her patience is a whole lot thinner than the crust of dust on Sally's dresser.

Several times, Karen has come within a hairsbreadth of a "Sally pile" to confronting her roommate about the problem.

But each time she stopped short, remembering that Christians —especially sanctified ones—are supposed to be long-suffering.

What are Karen's responsibilities to herself and to Sally? Should Karen discuss the problem with Sally? And if so, how?

David Augsburger has a few choice words for the long-suffering Karens of our day.

Chapter 7

Caring Enough to Confront

by David Augsburger

Background Scripture: 1 Corinthians 13:4-7; Galatians 2:11-14; 5:14-15

A GOOD WORD: Caring.

A bad word: Confronting.

Together they provide the balance of love and power that lead to effective human relationships.

A third word: Care-fronting. A good word.

Care-fronting is offering genuine caring that bids another to grow. (To care is to welcome, invite, and support growth in another.)

Care-fronting is offering real confrontation that calls out new insight and understanding. (To confront effectively is to offer the maximum of useful information with the minimum of threat and stress.)

Care-fronting unites love and power. Care-fronting unifies concern for relationship with concerns for goals. So one can have something to stand for (goals) as well as someone to stand with (relationship) without sacrificing one for the other, or collapsing one into another. Thus one can love powerfully and be powerfully loving. These are not contradictory. They are complimentary.

"That was a tasteless thing to do, just like your mother . . ." your husband mutters over dinner. You swallow twice at food gone flat, freeze into angry silence, get up from the table. (Familiar routine. He cuts. You retreat to lick the wound.)

You see in his eyes that he knows your next move—retreat

67

to the bedroom, an evening and night of cold, withdrawn anger. When you feel rejected, you reject.

"What's the point in running?" you ask yourself. "The longer I brood, the more I hurt. One of these times I'll tell him just how I feel."

Now is the time, you decide. Your feelings rush out. "When you criticize me like that, I feel rejected. I hurt. I usually run. But what I really want is to get around the wall between us and be able to feel close to you again. And I want you to respect me as me. I am not my mother. I am who I am." He's looking surprised. He's not used to hearing you describe your feelings so clearly. He's seldom heard you say what you really want.

Care-fronting is the way to communicate with both impact and respect, with truth and love.

"Speaking the truth in love" is *the way* to mature right relationships.

Care-fronting has a unique view of conflict. Conflict is natural, normal, neutral, and sometimes even delightful. It can turn into painful or disastrous ends, but it doesn't need to. Conflict is neither good nor bad, right nor wrong. Conflict simply is. How we view, approach, and work through our differences does—to a large extent—determine our whole life pattern. There are multiple views.

I might view conflict as *a given,* as a fixed matter of fate, explaining, "We just can't get along—we're incompatible—we'll never understand each other—that's all there is to it," then my life pattern would be one of avoiding threat and going my own safe, secure, well-armored way.

I could see conflict as *crushing.* "If we clash, I'll be judged—I'll be rejected—our friendship will fall through," then my life pattern would be acting the nice guy, quickly giving in to keep things comfortable.

I could view conflict as *an inevitable issue* of right and wrong, "I owe it to you, to me, to others, to God, to defend my truth and show you your error." Then my life would be rigid, perhaps perfectionistic, and judgmental.

I might begin to see conflict as *a mutual difference* to be resolved by meeting each other halfway. "I'll come part way, you come part way. Let's cooperate, compromise, or put our heads together in some joint way." Then my life pattern will be mediating, meet-me-in-the-middle style of one-for-me-and-one-for-you cooperation.

I can come to see conflict as *natural, neutral, normal.* I may then be able to see the difficulties we experience as tensions in relationships and honest differences in perspective that can be worked through by caring about each other and each confronting the other with truth expressed by love.

Each of these life patterns, or a combination of two, three, or four of the five, characterizes the conflict styles of most adults in your life. If you have them in the order listed, you are frequently frustrated, misunderstood, alienated, or just painfully confused about yourself and others. If your views are in reverse order, you're already chuckling and feeling good about the skills you either inherited or learned for resolving conflict. New skills can be learned. You'll add at least one by the end of this chapter.

"He's stealing me blind," you say, numb with anger. "Over $300 must have come in across the counter today, and his cash register ticket shows $175."

"Of all the stupid blunders, going into partnership with my brother-in-law has got to be the all-time winner," you say. Opening your pharmacy together had seemed so right. But in the first nine months you've barely turned a profit.

"The rat. He's been pocketing the cash, ringing up no-sales, or avoiding the register altogether." Whatever the system, he's picking you clean.

"I'll get him. I'll fix his wagon good, the embezzler." Oh, but you can't. It'll hurt your sister more than him, and she's just pulling away from a long depression.

"I'll shut up and get out. He can buy my half and have the whole thing—debt, mortgage, and all—right in his inadequate lap." Not so easy. Your home was mortgaged too for the operating capital. You're in all the way. To get out, you'll have to let him know you know.

"I'll give in and just sit on it for the time being. I'll wait for the auditor to catch it, or for him to hang himself by getting even more greedy." (Maybe if I give him a bonus, or commend him more for his work it will make him unbearably guilty.)

"I'll go halfway, I'll go along with him for a while, not say a thing, just stick so close he'll have to play fair." But breathing down his neck as you peer over his shoulder is a temporary compromise solution. You can't be there all the time.

"I've got to confront him with the goods. There's no other way out of the mess. But how do I do it?"

The five options: (1) I'll get him; (2) I'll get out; (3) I'll give in; (4) I'll meet you halfway; or (5) I care enough to confront, are the basic alternatives open in most conflict situations.

1. *"I'll get him"* is the I-win-you-lose-because-I'm-right-you're-wrong position in conflict. From this viewpoint, the attitude toward conflict is that the issues are all quite clear and simple. Someone is right—totally right, and someone is wrong—completely wrong. This win-lose stance uses all power and little or no love. Goal is valued above relationship. "My way is the only way," the person feels.

2. *"I'll get out"* is the I'm-uncomfortable-so-I'll-withdraw stance toward conflict. The viewpoint here is that conflicts are hopeless, people cannot be changed; we either overlook them or withdraw. Conflicts are to be avoided at all costs. When they threaten, get out of their way.

Withdrawal has its advantages if instant safety is the all-important thing. But it is a way out of conflict, not a way through. And a way out is no way at all.

In this lose-lose stance everyone loses. There is no risk of power, no trusting love. "Show me to the nearest exit," the person requests over the shoulder. It's a no-way or any-way response of flight.

3. *"I'll give in"* is the I'll-yield-to-be-nice-since-I-need-your-friendship approach. This perspective on conflict says that differences are disastrous. If they come out into the open, anything can happen. Anything evil, that is. It's far better to be nice, to submit, to go along with the other's demands and stay friends.

Yielding to keep contact will serve you well in many situations. But as a rule, it falls short. You become a doormat. A nice guy or gal. Frustrated. Yet smiling. The more tense and tight on the inside, the more generous and submissive on the outside.

4. *"I'll meet you halfway"* is the I-have-only-half-the-truth-and-I-need-your-half position. The attitude is one of creative compromise. Conflict is natural, and everyone should be willing to come part way in an attempt to resolve things. A willingness to give a little will lead to a working solution that is satisfactory to everyone.

Compromise is a gift to human relationships. We move forward on the basis of thoughtful, careful consensus and compromise in most decisions in conflict. But it calls for at least a partial sacrifice of deeply held views and goals, which may cost all of us the loss of the best to reach the good of agreement.

When we begin with a decision to compromise, we run the risk that my half of the truth added to your half may not give us the whole truth and nothing but the truth. We may have two half-truths. Or the combination may produce a whole untruth. Only when we care enough to tussle with truth can we test, retest, refine, and perhaps find more of it through our working at it seriously.

5. *"I care enough to confront"* is the I-want-relationship-and-I-also-want-honest-integrity position. Conflict is viewed as neutral (neither good nor bad) and natural (neither to be avoided nor short-circuited). Working through differences by giving clear messages of "I care" and "I want," which both care and confront, is most helpful.

71

This is interpersonal communication at its best. Caring—I want to stay in respectful relationships with you, *and* confronting—I want you to know where I stand and what I'm feeling, needing, valuing, and wanting.

Caring	Confronting
I care about our relationship.	I feel deeply about the issue at stake.
I want to hear your view.	I want to clearly express mine.
I want to respect your insights.	I want respect for mine.
I trust you to be able to handle my honest feelings.	I want you to trust me with yours.
I promise to stay with the discussion until we've reached an understanding.	I want you to keep working with me until we've reached a new understanding.
I will not trick, pressure, manipulate, or distort the difference.	I want your unpressured, clear, honest view of our differences.
I give you my loving, honest respect.	I want your caring-confronting response.

Of the five options in conflict situations—(1) I win—you lose; (2) I want out, I'll withdraw; (3) I'll give in for good relations; (4) I'll meet you halfway; (5) I can care and confront—the last is the most effective, the most truly loving, the most growth-promoting for human relationships. But often it will not be the starting point but the long-term goal.

When another comes on all "I win—you lose," it may be appropriate to respond with an "I'll give in for good relations" until the immediate storm is past. Then you can move back to an "I can care and confront" discussion.

When another responds immediately with an "I want out—I withdraw" attitude, choosing to work toward a compromise or a temporary focus on relationships can be appropriate for the moment to affirm your deep interest in continuing friendship.

But moving back to care-confront openness as soon as possible is important to you both.

Rigid fixation in any one style or exaggerated dependence on any one behavior will seldom be effective. The ability to respond in varied ways and the flexibility to match one's response to the shape a conflict is taking, are crucial skills to be added to year by year.

As a model of the ability to respond genuinely and appropriately with both love and power in balance, two millennia of Christians have looked to the confrontive, caring, and creative relationships modeled by Jesus of Nazareth. When examining His responses to various situations by using the language of conflict styles, one is immediately struck by His willingness to use any and all of the five as appropriate to His goals of redemptive compassion.

When the less-than-friendly hometown people of Nazareth rejected His message of confronting love, He chose to withdraw (see Luke 4:1-30). He cut off conversation and debate with the Pharisees when the point of clear rejection had arrived (see John 11:45-57).

Jesus was also free to act in an "I win—you lose" manner when this was the way to clearest understanding. He confronted the hucksters and hustlers in the Temple on win-lose terms (see Mark 11:11-19). Or read His clear statements to the religious leaders in Matthew 23, given after they had willed and arranged for His death.

At His arrest, during His interrogation, throughout His trial, in His unjust beating, and even through His execution, Jesus chose to submit to the anger of others, absorb it, and speak back the words of forgiveness, grace, and acceptance.

But no one has cared and confronted with greater effectiveness or more simple clarity than did Jesus.

To the would-be executioners of an accused adulteress, Jesus listened, waiting to hear their persistent questioning. *Caring.* Then He said, "Let the one among you who has never sinned throw the first stone at her." *Confrontation.*

To the woman, He said, "'Where are they all—did no one condemn you?' ... 'No one, sir.' 'Neither do I condemn you.'" *Warm, understandable care.* "Go away now and do not sin again." *Clear, unmistakable confrontation* (John 8:7, 10-11, Phillips).

In this letter to Christians at Ephesus, Paul described the nature of Christian maturity as modeled in Jesus' own integration of truth and love:

> So shall we all at last attain to the unity inherent in our faith and our knowledge of the Son of God—to mature manhood, measured by nothing less than the full stature of Christ. ... Let us speak the truth in love; so shall we fully grow up into Christ *(Ephesians 4:13, 15, NEB).*

John summarized the presence of God among us in Jesus with these same words.

> So the Word became flesh; he came to dwell among us, and we saw his glory, ... full of grace and truth *(John 1:14, NEB).*

Truth with love brings healing.

Truth told in love enables us to grow.

Truth in love produces change.

Truth and love are the two necessary ingredients for any relationship with integrity. Love—because all positive relationships begin with friendship, appreciation, respect. And truth—because no relationship of trust can long grow from dishonesty, deceit, betrayal; it springs up from the solid stuff of integrity.

"Confrontation plus caring brings growth just as judgment plus grace brings salvation," says Howard Clinebell, Jr., a well-known pastoral counselor.

These are the two arms of genuine relationship: Confrontation with truth; affirmation with love.

I grow most rapidly when supported with the arm of loving respect, then confronted with the arm of clear honesty. Confronting and caring stimulate growth.

This is how God relates to us. When we speak of God's relationship with man we have historically used other words.

Judgment and grace lead to salvation.

God's judgment—radical honesty about truth—confronts us with the demands of disciplined maturity.

God's grace—undeserved love—reaches out to accept and affirm us at the point we know ourselves to be unacceptable.

Judgment cuts, even kills. If God dealt with us only in judgment, who could stand? If God reached out to us only in love, it would be a cheap grace without integrity, mere divine permissiveness. "Anything goes" as far as heaven is concerned? Not so!

Judgment blended with grace.

Confrontation matched with caring.

Truth spoken in love.

Honesty, truth, trust, and love, these all interlock and intertwine in the biblical statements on relationships.

Condensed by permission from *Caring Enough to Confront,* by David Augsburger. Copyright by Herald Press, Scottsdale, PA 15683.

Temptation:

A Scene from Life

Sam likes women. Always has.

He was raised with three older sisters. And now, as a married father, he still likes women.

Sam and his wife have enjoyed marriage for about a dozen years, and they're both solid Christians, active in a holiness church.

Throughout the past 12 years, Sam continued to enjoy the company of women both at work and at church. And sometimes he would even stand back and admire God's handiwork. This never seemed to threaten his marriage or his faith. But lately he has caught himself looking with greater intensity. And fleeting fantasies are not as fleeting as they used to be.

All this really has him bothered. He loves his wife and family, along with the Lord, and would never want to hurt them.

But the temptations are surging, and his guilt is near flood stage.

Is this degree of temptation a sign that Sam is losing his Christianity? Charles R. Swindoll has a few enlightening things to say to Sam and others like him who are battling with all kinds of temptation every day.

Chapter 8

How to Battle Temptation

by Charles R. Swindoll

Background Scripture: Genesis 39:1-8; James 1:13-15

MARK ANTHONY was known as the "silver-throated orator of Rome." He was a brilliant statesman, magnificent in battle, courageous, and strong. And he was handsome. As far as personal qualities are concerned, he could have become a world ruler. But he had the vulnerable and fatal flaw of moral weakness, so much so that on one occasion his personal tutor shouted into his face, "Oh, Marcus, oh, colossal child! Able to conquer the world, but unable to resist a temptation."

That indictment, I'm afraid, applies not just to Mark Anthony, and not just to the people of the unsaved world. If the truth were known, it is applicable to many in the evangelical ranks. We *all* face temptation, and it is a very real fact that many do not yet know how to resist it and overcome it when it appears.

Trials or Temptations? Knowing the Difference

There's a definite difference between *trials* and *temptations*. Trials are ordeals—tests of our faith. Normally, there is nothing immoral involved in experiencing a trial. A trial is a hardship, an ordeal. But it is generally not something that is evil or brought about by evil.

Take, for example, Job's trials. He lost his health, his family, his home, his business—he lost everything! But nothing immoral brought about Job's problems; it was a test—in fact a severe series of tests.

Or look at a depressed Elijah under the juniper tree. When his life was threatened, he went away to hide and pleaded with God. Nothing immoral or evil caused Elijah's experience of depression. It was a test, a hardship, an ordeal.

But when we get to temptation, it's different. That is why in James 1:13, the verse includes the word "tempted." Although it is the same Greek word we have read in verses 1 through 12, in the writer's mind it meant something different. It changed from the ordeal to the idea of soliciting evil.

A glance at your dictionary will inform you that temptation is "the act of enticement to do wrong, by promise of pleasure or gain." That's right! Temptation motivates you to be bad by promising something good. Isn't that just like the devil?

Four Facts About Temptation

There are four basic principles regarding temptation. Before we deal with how to handle it, let's get those principles down. They all lie within three verses of James 1.

"Let no one say when he is tempted, 'I am being tempted by God'; for God cannot be tempted by evil, and He Himself does not tempt anyone. But each one is tempted when he is carried away and enticed by his own lust. Then when lust has conceived, it gives birth to sin; and when sin is accomplished, it brings forth death" (James 1:13-15, NASB).

(1) *Temptation is inevitable.* James did not say, "Let no one say, *if* he is tempted . . ." He said, "*when* he is tempted." And there's a difference.

It would be wonderful if we could live without facing temptations. But the simple fact is we cannot.

(2) *Temptation is never directed by God.* He permits it, to be sure, but He never directs it. God does not direct us into sin. Notice, in James 1:13, that God cannot be tempted by evil, and God does not tempt.

God is not even *indirectly* engaged in bringing us into sin. To be sure, God certainly permits the events of our lives to take place as they do. But when we yield to the temptations that appear before us, God has had absolutely no part in that act. Instead, it is you and I who have disobeyed and given in to the temptation.

(3) *Temptation is an individual matter.* Nothing outside ourselves is strong enough—not even Satan—to cause us to sin. *Sin takes place when we agree to the temptation and follow it.* It takes an agreement on our part. Not until I individually involve myself does sin take place. Up to that point I am safe and pure.

Let me illustrate it this way. I have an attorney friend who works in conjunction with the Federal Reserve Bank in another city. He made the mistake of taking me there one afternoon. We walked in together and were checked all over. (You know how thorough they are if you've ever been there.) Behind a large section of bulletproof glass are people who do nothing but count money.

I asked him, "How can they stand it behind there?"

He said, "Everything is fine if they remember their job is only to count pieces of paper. If they begin to concentrate on what those pieces of paper represent, then we have problems."

Open doors to sin face us all each day. The person centered on Christ and His righteousness says, "Nothing doing," and willfully walks away. The person intent on satisfying his own desires for sin says, "Oh, I just can't help myself," and walks in. The good news for the Christian is that by the power of the Holy Spirit, *we can help it!*

(4) *Temptation that leads to sin always follows the same overall process.* Pay close attention:

Step 1: The bait is dropped.

Step 2: The inner desire is attracted to that bait.

Step 3: Sin occurs when we yield—when we bite the bait.

Step 4: Sin results in tragic consequences—we end up hooked and fried.

I'm using these vivid and analogous terms because of James' terminology. Watch what he wrote:

> But each one is tempted when he is carried away and enticed by his own lust. Then when lust has conceived, it gives birth to sin; and when sin is accomplished, it brings forth death *(James 1:14-15)*.

The word "entice" (v. 14) is a fishing term. When you fish, you've got to provide a bait that interests and entices a fish. Where I live, fish like shrimp. You put a juicy little shrimp on the hook and try to keep him alive so he keeps snapping and dancing, just as if he's swimming, and you cast out into the ocean. A big gulf trout cannot resist it, if he sees it. If you handle things just right, you've got a sure strike. Why? Because you have chosen a bait that interests the fish.

I don't know how fish think, but they probably look and think something like, "Wow, that looks great!" And when that fish leaves his hiding place for the bait, he's as good as caught.

So are we.

As long as we remain obedient to the Lord, drawing our strength and our delight from Him, the evil system around us can drop all sorts of bait and it won't seriously interest us. Oh, it's there. But our Lord's Word and power are stronger and more important to us than anything out there.

But when we choose not to obey God and slip out after the bait, we're as good as gone.

Perhaps you're wondering how to say no consistently. Look at Genesis 39 for the classic means to handle temptation.

Here is a handsome single man, Joseph, alone in Potiphar's home. And Potiphar's wife has a lustful desire for this man, and says, "Lie with me." Now, that's what I'd call dropping the bait! Nothing subtle about Mrs. Potiphar!

But Joseph refused. He took off. He ran like mad. By the way, there's a name for folks who linger and try to reason with lust: *victim*.

Practical Ways to Handle Temptation

It can be done! Look, we have made resisting temptation some mystical, unreachable, unattainable talent reserved either for the very old or the very pious. *Baloney!* Saying *no* is something all of us who belong to Christ can do. There's nothing magical about it.

Let me break this practice down into four workable, practical principles to follow.

(1) *Counteract temptation. Do not tolerate it.* Let's face it: We play around with things that make us weak. Let me get specific. If you are weakened by certain motion pictures that bring before your eyes things that build desires within you that you can't handle, then you're not counteracting sin and temptation. You're tolerating it. You're fertilizing it. You're prompting it.

If the newsstand is something you can't handle, stay away from it! If you feed your mind on the garbage of "national magazines" (and I mean even the more popular ones) and cannot handle those things, stay away from them. Quit clucking your tongue and shaking your head as you linger over the pages.

Learn from Joseph. Run!

The words of Dag Hammarskjöld—secretary general to the United Nations in the mid and late 1950s—throb with wisdom:

"You cannot play with the animal in you without becoming wholly animal, play with falsehood without forfeiting your right to truth, play with cruelty without losing your sensitivity of mind. He who wants to keep his garden tidy doesn't reserve a plot for weeds."*

(2) *Use the right resistance.* I'll give you some examples, for not all temptations are handled the same in the Scriptures.

When lust or sensual sins are mentioned in the New Testament, we are told to "flee," to run, to get away.

Let me share with you an experience I had in the oriental city of Naha on Okinawa. I used to take a little bus down to the place where a group of men in the military gathered for Bible study. I got off the bus at a particular corner and had to walk about six blocks, since this was as far as the bus would take us. Okinawa was unique—it had more bars per mile than any island in the South Pacific. There was just one sensual opportunity after another along the way. Each joint was an open door to lustful satisfaction.

I walked straight ahead, looking neither to the right nor to the left.

Moreover, I have discovered that what worked over in Okinawa works in California. When your eyes turn to the right or to the left, you're on your way to grabbing the bait. It is the *second* glance that leads one into sin.

If you are tempted to gossip and lie, God says there's an answer to that. Avoid it. You say, "Well, that's one way." No, that's the *only* way! A bridle isn't the answer for gossip—you need a muzzle. If it's confidential, if you can't trace the source of the information, if you don't have the OK from the person you are talking about, then keep your mouth shut!

(3) *Remind yourself that the final pain will soon erase the temporary pleasure.* That's exactly what Moses did when he chose to walk with God rather than to become absorbed in Egypt's life-style.

"By faith Moses, when he had grown up, refused to be called the son of Pharaoh's daughter; choosing rather to en-

82

dure ill-treatment with the people of God, than to enjoy the passing pleasures of sin" (Hebrews 11:24-25).

"The passing pleasures of sin." What an eloquent expression—and true! Is sin pleasureable? You bet! It's so pleasureable that people will risk their reputations to taste its flavor. In doing so, all the efforts of our minds to alert us to sin's dangers are neutralized. We turn off the internal warnings as we turn on the desire.

(4) *Control your thought life through the memorized Word.* When the devil launched his full-scale attack against Jesus (Matthew 4:1-11), our Lord withstood temptation by using the Scriptures. "It is written . . . it is written . . . it is written!"

When the Word of God is stored up in our minds, it stands ready to strike. No weapon can stand against the truth.

Is this for real? I mean, will it actually work? I can testify by my personal experience that it really does. It *has,* time and again.

I was in Canada, months ago. I had been away from home eight days, and there were two more to go—a weekend. I was lonely and having a pity-party for myself at supper —alone. I bought a newspaper, thumbed though the sports section, and found nothing but hockey—the favorite of Canadians but not mine. I heaved a sigh and walked toward the elevator. En route, I heard a couple of young women talking and laughing as they used the hotel phone in the lobby.

I smiled as I passed by and a few steps later punched the "up" elevator button. I got on. So did the two ladies. I punched "6." They didn't reach for the row of buttons, so I asked, "What floor?" One looked at me rather sensually and said, "How about six? Do you have any plans?"

We were all alone on an elevator. In Canada. I was flattered, to be honest, since most folks don't usually mistake me for Robert Redford or James Garner. These women were available, and I was lonely. On that trip from the lobby to the sixth floor, I had an extremely significant decision to make . . . the bait had been dropped.

Do you know what immediately flashed into my mind? My wife and four children? No, not at first. My position and reputation? No, not then. The possibility of being seen or set up? No.

God gave me an instant visual replay of Galatians 6:7 (NASB):

> Do not be deceived, God is not mocked; for whatever a man sows, this he will also reap.

and Ephesians 6:11 (NASB):

> Put on the full armor of God, that you may be able to stand firm against the schemes of the devil.

and Romans 6:11-12:

> Even so consider yourselves to be dead to sin, but alive to God in Christ Jesus. Therefore do not let sin reign in your mortal body that you should obey its lusts.

During that elevator lift, the memorized Word flew to my rescue. Right on time.

As I looked back at the two, I replied, "I've got a full evening planned already; I'm really not interested." They looked at me like I was Mork from Ork as I stepped off the elevator (and they stayed on!). I walked to my room, suddenly grateful for the overcoming power of God's Book.

In a quaint little village north of Pittsburgh, a shining new red brick building was built, designed to be the new city hall. It also housed the police and fire departments. It was a small building, but the people loved it.

In a matter of just a few months, however, the building began to show some obvious cracks. The windows would not close all the way. Before too many weeks, the doors were ajar and would not shut. The floor buckled. Finally, the sidewalk in front of the building cracked. In a period of less than a year, the building had to be condemned.

A careful, expensive investigation was made, and it was found that deep below the surface they had built too near some mining work. The mining had weakened the foundational area, so that slowly but surely, this building was cracking, shifting, sinking, dropping, and breaking into pieces because of a flaw underneath.

The moral of this isn't difficult to grasp. If you piddle around with temptation long enough, playing with it, lingering near its bait over and over and over again, then down in the heart and life of your character there will be permanent damage. That vulnerable flaw or weakness will lead to serious moral damage that you cannot imagine.

Come to terms with this now ... or you will regret it later.

---

*Dag Hammarskjöld, *Markings* (New York: Alfred A. Knopf, 1964), 15.

Reprinted by permission of Thomas Nelson Publishers, from the book *Three Steps Forward, Two Steps Back.* Copyright 1980 by Charles R. Swindoll.

Sex:

A Scene from Life

There are two men in Mandy's life, though she probably wouldn't put it that way.

She loves her husband. But lately, she has found herself strangely drawn to her boss at the office. He's a caring and sensitive man that Mandy liked right from the first, when she started working with him three years ago.

But lately, she has felt drawn to him physically. And when she lays in bed at night, she often falls asleep dreaming about romantic encounters with her dark-haired, robust employer.

And for the past couple months, nearly every time she made love with her husband, she pretended, at least part of the time, that she was with her boss.

Though she would not dare tell her husband about this, she truly feels there is nothing wrong with this fantasizing. After all, she is a Christian and would never consider really having an affair. Besides, this romantic daydreaming is normal and private—it hurts no one, and it has actually seemed to improve her sex life with her husband.

Ed Robinson has a few words of counsel for Mandy, and for anyone else who struggles with what it means to live a holy life in our sex-oriented age.

Chapter 9

Sex: When the Hunger Takes Control

by Ed Robinson

Background Scripture: Colossians 3:1-17

SEX.

The very sound of the word stirs up all kinds of thoughts. Sex has worked its way into almost every part of our culture. No matter how much we wish the sleazy side of sex would go away and hide, it isn't going to.

I woke up one morning awhile back and after having my devotions and daily bowl of Cheerios, I switched on the television and watched a popular talk-show host praise a new comedy sitcom featuring two homosexual males in a struggle for identity and for acceptance by their family and friends.

The program was interrupted by a commercial message encouraging me to buy a brand of toothpaste that would improve my sex appeal (as if it needed help).

That was immediately followed by a short preview extolling the "spicy" new shows of the "sizzling" fall season.

Outside my apartment I was greeted by a bulletin board advertisement for a "straight" female who wanted to share an apartment with another "straight" female. I remember when she would have said, "Nice girl looking for a roommate" and everyone would have understood what she meant.

A short drive took me by the Blues Adult Bookstore, which bills itself as the "24-Hour Store for Adults."

Frankly, I'm glad I don't live in the Puritan Age with its monocolored clothes, high collars, long sleeves, and prudish conversation. I appreciate the openness of our modern era which has produced many fine Christian books dealing with the complexities of midlife, sex in marriage, and Christian singleness to mention a few. But I don't feel completely comfortable with all this sexual freedom, or should I say sexual confusion? It's almost as if we are playing teeter-totter with our sexual identities. We have been parked on the ground at one extreme or the other for so long that we don't know what it is to balance modesty with the healthy, valid expression of our sexual selves.

And where does that put me, a Christian who has committed his life to the Lordship of Jesus Christ? I can't even go through the normal activities of a morning without facing a bombardment of sexual innuendos. Can I really maintain a commitment to holy living in the middle of all this? Can I keep my thoughts and actions pure while voices all around me cry, "Be free!" "You're the only one who matters," "If it feels good, do it!"

God's command in Leviticus is still the mandate for today. "Be holy for I am holy." Likewise, the call of the apostle Paul has not lost its intensity.

> It is God's will that you should be sanctified: that you should avoid sexual immorality; that each of you should learn to control his own body in a way that is holy and honorable, not in passionate lust like the heathen, who do not know God; and that in this matter no one should wrong his brother or take advantage of him. The Lord will punish men for all such sins, as we have already told you and warned you. For God did not call us to be impure, but to live a holy life. Therefore, he who rejects this instruction does not reject man but God, who gives you his Holy Spirit *(1 Thessalonians 4:3-8)*.

Sex is a gift of God to man to accomplish great purposes. Some of those purposes, like biological reproduction, are obvious and understood by most everyone. Other purposes are not so clear. They have been muddled by ignorance, selfishness, and perversion, so they can't be seen through the natural eyes of man. These purposes come from a biblical understanding of what God wants for mankind. In other words, the purposes are spiritual and cannot be grasped from a simply physical perspective.

Let me put it another way. The pleasure of sex is not only

in the feeling, but also in the meaning. If we are to understand God's great purposes in giving His creation the good gift of sex (everything God created is good, 1 Timothy 4:3) then we must take a look at sex from God's point of view.

God gifted us with sexual identities so we might celebrate our humanity. The value of the person is at the heart of any sexual expression. The story of the creation of Adam and Eve is the account of two people created for fellowship with God and with each other. It was a celebration of life!

> So God created man in his own image, in the image of God he created him; male and female he created them *(Genesis 1:27)*.
>
> For this reason a man will leave his father and mother and be united to his wife, and they will become one flesh. The man and his wife were both naked, and they felt no shame *(Genesis 2:24-25)*.

The scriptures are loaded with instructions guiding our relationships with people. Paul's Epistles to the churches are packed with guidelines on how to relate to others (spouses, children, employers, believers, friends, even enemies). Read Colossians 3 for a powerful example. It is in this understanding of relationships that we begin to see the relationship between God's gift of sex and the value of people.

When I first became attracted to my wife, Nancy, I was proud to be seen with her (and still am). Her beauty made me look good to everyone on the college campus where we met. Believe me, I needed the help! But after I had matured a bit in our relationship, the focus of my feelings and wants changed. This was particularly evident in our sex life after we had married. I was beginning to understand the value of this wonderful person God had allowed me to love and cherish.

The current "no commitment" sexual relationships, portrayed in the media and practiced in the bedrooms of many, simply betray the gift of humanity God has given to each of us. We need to set our sights high for sexual expression, not below God's intended use. "Since, then, you have been raised with Christ, set your hearts on things above, where Christ is seated at the right hand of God. Set your mind on things above, not on earthly things" (Colossians 3:1-2).

That is all well and good, you say. But why do we have such dynamic urges and thought lives concerning sex. Congratulations! We're human! The ability to have those urges and think those thoughts are God's special gift to us. The challenge we face is in sexually expressing ourselves within the boundaries God has prescribed in His Word. Because the sexual drive is so dynamic, it is one chief area Satan will use to attack us and break down our commitment to holy living.

God's Word concerning sexual purity is clear: sexual activity that degrades the humanity of others is wrong. Expressions of love are to be guided by a caring, giving, nurturing attitude. This principle applies even *within* the sexual relationship of a husband and wife. Remember 1 Thessalonians 4:6: "And that in this matter [sexual immorality] no one should wrong his brother or take advantage of him."

Also, in God's grand design for sex, the act of sexual union is to be experienced only within the security of the total commitment of marriage. In the beginning of a long discussion on marriage in 1 Corinthians 7, Paul clearly says that the marriage relationship is to be monogamous and that sexual faithfulness is a part of that arrangement.

In light of these simple biblical principles, a look at the concepts of temptation, thought life, and sin is in order. A man, by his very nature, is sexually aroused by the sight of an attractive woman. This is not sin. It is human. A woman, on the other hand, is more generally moved by nonvisual signals; she can be attracted to a sensitive, caring man in her office, neighborhood, or church. This is not sin. It is human.

To be tempted by the thought of sexual encounters with that person *is still not sin*. It does not become sin until we have nurtured the thoughts to action, either in reality or in the fantasy world of our thoughts. Jesus compared thought life and reality when He said, "Anyone who looks at a woman lustfully has already committed adultery with her in his heart" (Matthew 5:28).

Most of us are not seriously and doggedly tempted to commit sexual immorality in our outward actions. We have either made a firm commitment to pure sexual expression or we're

deathly afraid of getting caught! But the thought life is a different story for us. Most of us are tempted at this point. And it's
easy to give in to the temptation to fantasize. It *appears* to be
so private. "It doesn't hurt anyone," we say. "After all, what
difference does it make?"

It makes a great deal of difference. Uncontrolled thought
life in sexual fantasy erodes our relationship with others, with
ourselves, and ultimately with God. Sexual fantasies erode our
relationship with others because the fantasies force us to think
of people as sex toys built for our selfish, personal pleasure—
not as people to be served and nurtured. Nothing could be more
dehumanizing or unchristlike. And concerning the privacy of
the matter, eventually our actions are going to betray our
hearts.

Uncontrolled thought life also degenerates our self-worth
by robbing us of the sense of guilt-free joy and fulfillment God
has created for us. The sense of wonder and discovery that we
find in marriage is cheapened by the false images and expectations of fantasy. It takes experience to achieve the best in sexual expression with a marriage partner. If we create an unreal,
inhumanly ideal picture of what that expression should be like,
we rob ourselves of the happiness of that union. It is like taking
a picture of a shadow, instead of the real thing.

Finally, lustful thoughts jeopardize our relationship with
God, because impure thoughts are acts of disobedience against
His standard of holy living. That is not to say that uncontrolled
sexual fantasies are beyond God's grace and forgiveness. Most
of the New Testament Christians were converted from a culture
that was sexually immoral inside and out. The point is that
sexual immorality, real or fantasy, is not acceptable behavior in
the eyes of God.

So what can we do when sexual fantasies invade our
thoughts? Earl Wilson, a Christian psychologist, recommends
tracing the chain of events that leads to the unhealthy thought
patterns. Once that chain is revealed, we should break the
chain by substituting a different activity.

For example, let's say that every Sunday afternoon you
read the TV section of the newspaper, looking for "spicy" pro-

grams you might watch during the coming week. You realize that when you pick up that supplement, it's going to direct you into a video world of lustful fantasies.

You might try breaking this chain by not reading that section of the paper. Instead, begin to cultivate a habit of reading something else on Sunday afternoons.

Temptation, even in the area of sex, is not sin until it is nurtured into action by our own will and desire. But when it comes to life it needs the forgiveness and cleansing that only the blood of Jesus Christ can provide.

God loves His best creation, man and woman, so much that He has equipped us with the ability to experience one of life's most meaningful moments. As I already said, the real pleasure of sex is not primarily in the feeling. It is in the meaning. And the real meaning comes only after we understand God's great purposes for sex:

1. Sex is an expression of the spiritual unity of husband and wife. Ephesians 5 uses the comparison of Christ and the Church to clarify the marriage relationship. Just as Christ and the Church are one, so must the husband and wife be one. Sex is an outward expression of that spiritual oneness.

2. Sex is a means of communicating commitment. I have already mentioned the concept of faithfulness in marriage. Sex in marriage is a way of saying that commitment is still very real.

3. Sex is a means of showing deep affection. One of the beauties of God's gift of sex is in the opportunity it affords one marriage partner to say to the other, "I love you and give myself to you." Reading the Song of Solomon in this light brings a new meaning to that portion of God's Word.

4. Sex is for procreation. Billy Graham once said to a gathering of college students, "Sex is all right; without it none of us would be here." God commanded Adam and Eve to be fruitful and multiply. Sex is the means of that multiplication.

5. Sex is for recreation, or, more simply, fun. Proverbs 5:18 speaks of rejoicing in the wife of your youth. Sex is meant to be an exhilarating, pleasurable experience within the framework of marriage.

So, sex is for much more than the physical satisfaction of a biological urge. God has placed the sex drive in men and women so they might express and experience *all* these five aspects. The five are not a smorgasbord from which we can pick and choose. They are all important, especially the spiritual ones of unity, commitment, and affection. These five are at the heart of what it means to "make love." These are the grand design of God.

God has given us a beautiful gift to express some beautiful values. Unfortunately, our secular culture has cheapened the gift by focusing on the single aspect of pleasure. And our culture has even distorted that to mean self-satisfaction. Consequently, too many Christians have been caught up in this, while others have overreacted to it. And as a result, the gift has lost much of its dynamic for even those of us who call ourselves "holy."

God grant us the wisdom to recapture this gift He has so wonderfully given us. May we use the gift for its intended use, and enjoy it in the spirit in which it was given.

Ambition:

A Scene from Life

Loretta is the first woman to make it to the executive wing in the company she works for.

She was shocked when the announcement came that she would head up the public relations section. She was shocked not only because she was a woman, but also because everyone knew she was a Christian.

One of the first things she did was to promote Tim, a talented artist, to help her as art director. They were a team that couldn't miss, she thought. And she seemed to be right.

For two years, they worked together and collected rave reviews for their creative work. Then it happened. Her art director accepted a higher paying job back East, where the family of Tim and his wife lived.

Loretta was furious. "Where am I going to find another art director like Tim?" she complained. She felt Tim's decision was nothing short of a betrayal that would certainly endanger her candidacy for the vice presidential slot coming open next year.

Loretta needs some counseling about the tension between her ambitions and the needs and ambitions of others. Cecil R. Paul will give her some guidance about the place of ambition in the life of a Christian.

Chapter 10

Ambitious, but Christian

by Cecil R. Paul

Background Scripture: Matthew 25:14-30; Philippians 2:1-11

WHEN SOME PEOPLE think about the word "ambition" they remember Sheriff Andy Taylor on the old "Andy Griffith Show."

You may recall that Sheriff Taylor seemed to be totally void of ambition. He was content to serve in Mayberry; he had no aspirations to move up the ladder into a law enforcement job in the big city of Raleigh.

Was the sheriff really lacking in ambition? What is ambition, anyhow?

My dictionary calls it a strong desire to reach a particular objective; specifically, a drive to achieve things like fame, wealth, and power. To a Christian, this sounds pretty negative. But the dictionary adds that there are both positive and negative implications to the word "ambition."

Falling under the category of ambition is the aspiring person, who seeks lofty goals and is willing to strive after them. And there is the enterprising person, who invests time and energy in projects that are important to him. There is also the competitive person, who seeks to surpass others.

All three of these make up different parts of the word "ambition." And all three are preached and highly valued within most circles of our society. In fact, if we are caught without them, we are branded as lazy, lacking motivation and strength of character.

Ambition has been vital to the development of civilization, for without it the wheel would not have been invented. Yet the tension between our ambitions and the needs and ambitions of others raises some important questions for the Christian. Just how does ambition fit into the Christian life?

The media bombards us with this goal: live successful lives. And this kind of success or "good life" is interpreted in terms of this world's values. So, to be ambitious means look out for number one, never be content with what you've got, and always seek attention and recognition. The hero-figures for our day have become entertainers, athletes, and other center-stage people.

The Call to Investment

The teachings of Jesus are filled with stories encouraging the believer to invest his talents. In fact, the following words of Jesus indicate that people will be judged on the basis of their investment of talents. "Well done, good and faithful servant! You have been faithful with a few things; I will put you in charge of many things. Come and share your master's happiness" (Matthew 25:21). In verse 29, Jesus goes on to say, "For everyone who has will be given more, and he will have an abundance. Whoever does not have, even what he has will be taken from him."

Unfortunately, we fail to interpret these stories on the basis of the context and purpose. The intended spiritual lessons are lost as we interpret these teachings in terms of our individual this-worldly ambitions. Jesus is talking about kingdoms, ultimate values, and the meaning of commitment. He is teaching principles that will enable us to lead full lives as members of caring communities. The word "investment" is important in relationship to ambition. The key questions we need to face are: What do I ultimately value? What am I primarily invested in and what is the purpose of that investment? If I am primarily invested in possessions and power for personal success and the establishment of my own kingdom, then my ambitions are in radical tension with the teachings of Jesus. When ambition becomes focused on building barns and the filling of them as an expression of my own territory, power, and recognition, then I become as the rich man.

"But God said to him, 'You fool! This very night your life will be demanded from you. Then who will get what you have prepared for yourself?'" (Luke 12:20). The context helps us enlarge on this, for Jesus then says, "Life is more than food, and the body more than clothes" (Luke 12:23).

The way to the top of the ladder usually means abusing others, or perhaps ignoring them and their needs. The subtleties of successful living have even crept into the church community, as we begin to value people on the basis of *appearance, performance, power, position,* and *possession.*

A board member of one holiness church started to bring a scrubby-looking neighbor of his to the church services. After several weeks of this, the board member was told to stop bringing "that kind of person" into the church.

"And if I don't stop?"

"Then you'll be removed from the church board."

The argument the church leaders made was that they wanted to be seen as a respected church in the community.

Ambition directed toward these selfish objectives is in radical tension with the teachings and example of Jesus and His disciples. It is carnal ambition that moves us into a state of separation or estrangement.

Our carnal behavior demonstrates we are *estranged from God,* having become our own gods with our own kingdoms. Our behavior and attitudes demonstrate we are *estranged from our neighbors,* in that they become means to our power, possessions, and success. It estranges us from others as we lead fragmented lives that will never know the ultimate joy of being a part of the kingdom of mutual love. Our carnal ambition *estranges us from ourselves,* as we become locked into the prison of these narrow limits to the meaning of life and wholeness. This idolatry of self leaves us with no resources or power beyond ourselves.

The Call to Stewardship

The key to understanding the place of ambition in the Christian life is to look at it in terms of stewardship. The word "investment" takes on a new meaning here. Rather than an investment in terms of my own gain, it becomes an investment of myself in loving God and my neighbor. If I build and fill barns, it is with that ultimate purpose in mind.

To be a good steward is to be ambitious for the kingdom of God. It means that I am moving beyond self-service to the full development of my skills as an expression of my commitment to God and the needs of others. Holy living is holistic living. It means the development of all of our individual and shared gifts to their fullest potential, for the good of all.

I was a young convert of 17 when I came under the influence of Anne and Henry Johnson. They demonstrated that we are not called to ambitions such as lofty positions and power of possessions. Though they had the professional roles and the means to self-indulge, they were models of service to others. They reached out into the poor and rural communities to touch the lives of children for Christ. Because of the Johnsons, hundreds of children were transported and nurtured into Sunday School and the activities of the church. Those seeds of service that were sown continue to impact the lives of people and their communities.

Paul confronts the issue of ambition a number of times, no doubt because he had an ongoing struggle with it himself. The concepts of crucifixion of self, self-denial, dying for Christ, were powerful expressions of Paul's confrontation with the issue of ambition. For Paul, ambition was seen in radical commitment of all of one's gifts, to achieve "the mind of Christ." This definition of ambition takes us way beyond personal gain and power or the competitive desire to do better than others.

Success, as a preoccupation, can be a heavy yoke. The thirst is not quenched, but, in fact, intensifies. Witness the tragic lives of many entertainers who, judging by the coverage they receive in magazines and television, have explored the upper limits of human ambition. The lessons we need to learn from them are that there are demonic powers operating in the area of ambition. These forces destroy us, just as surely as they destroy our relationships with others.

A problem we face is that it is natural and human to want to fulfill our potential in life. But how can we do this without going off the deep end of ambition?

Jesus gives us the model we need. He provides the essence of what it means to be ambitious. Paul summarized it when he challenged the Christian to pursue a value system dramatically different from the values of the world. He challenged us to consecrate ourselves by "having the mind of Christ."

Scott and Missy Skiles represent the call to service above self. They journeyed to the inner city of New York, leaving behind the security and comfortable relationships of family and friends in Kansas City. All this to minister to the inner city. As I write this, they are serving Christ and community through the Lamb's Club of Manhattan Church of the Nazarene. Their vision was to serve the people who have known the crush of loss, failure, and rejection. Their commitment to have the mind of Christ has taken them into the arena of human suffering.

Jan Lanham and I discuss the meaning of having the mind of Christ in our book *Choices: In Pursuit of Wholeness*. To have the mind of Christ is to know the power of His life-transforming love. Only then is the law fulfilled, because it is expressed not out of legal obligation, but from a changed perspective on self, others, and God. We do not love in order to meet some legal obligation. We love as a joyful response to God's love for us. This is our ambition. It is not to be in competition with others, whether in terms of secular success, or religious piety. It is to be in relationship to that person out of loving care.

One of the finest examples of a person having the mind of Christ is my wife, Judy, who works at the difficult task of negotiating educational services for the handicapped. This work demands great patience and wisdom as well as a vision of what can happen in the lives of the handicapped. Parents and teachers and the many professional people with whom Judy works are moved by her transparent love and investment in the lives of others. I find it interesting that her favorite stories are those of people who overcome handicaps and crises, turning them into the occasion for character building and spiritual development.

Having the mind of Christ causes us to have a healthy perspective of grace and mercy. In the Beatitudes, this new life in Christ is contrasted with the rejection of both the world and the religious community. Christian ambition is to accept in our hearts and then make real in our relationships these principles He taught us:

> Blessed are the poor in spirit
> Blessed are the meek
> Blessed are the merciful
> Blessed are the pure in heart

The Christian finds a new sense of worth through the power of God's grace working in his life. It is this grace and love that saves us from the sin of self-serving actions and attitudes. "Let this mind be in you, which was also in Christ Jesus" (Philippians 2:5, KJV) is followed by the challenge of "Do not think of yourself more highly than you ought" (Romans 12:3).

Paul goes on to admonish the believer. "Do not be proud, but be willing to associate with people of low position" (Romans 12:16). As recipients of God's grace and mercy, we become the channels of the same to others. In doing so, we are to judge others slowly and forgive them quickly, because we never outgrow our own need for God's grace.

Having the mind of Christ causes us to be peacemakers. "Blessed are the peacemakers: for they shall be called the children of God" (Matthew 5:9, KJV). The writer to the Hebrews expressed it this way: "Make every effort to live in peace with all men and to be holy; without holiness no one will see the Lord" (Hebrews 12:14). The focus of our ambition is to become actively engaged in making peace with others.

That certainly doesn't sound like the kind of ambition we see in our world. In fact, "peacemaker" is at the other end of the spectrum from the junior executive who steps on people in his climb toward the penthouse. And there is no peacemaking at work with the secretary in the clerical pool who bad-mouths the lead secretary in the hope of getting promoted into that slot.

Ambition, from the Christian point of view, is based on a value system that reflects the life and teachings of Jesus Christ. Rather than seeking my interests, my goals, my desires, I seek the mind of Christ.

To pursue the mind of Christ is to spend our time and energies in those activities that we believe reflect His values. One effective way to sort out our ambitions is to look at what we give most of our time and energy to in daily living. The following exercise is to help you in that process.

Revising Priorities

1. What are some of the areas of your life you would like to improve on as an expression of having the mind of Christ? Try to think of several specific activities or goals you would like to incorporate into your daily living. For example, you may feel there are skills and talents you have neglected to develop. List these. There may be relationships with some people that you would like to handle differently. Your ambition, then, would be to develop both your skills and handling of relationships with these people.

2. Review your daily and weekly investment of time and energy, in order to determine what your real life priorities seem to be. One way of doing this is to check your appointment book or your calendar to see what you gave priority to over the past week and month. If you do not keep a diary, calendar, or ap-

101

pointment book, this would be a good time to begin one in order to more effectively evaluate your time and energy. Regardless of this, try to determine what you have been giving your time and energy to over the past week and month. This includes what you are preoccupied with throughout your days.

3. List the forces that seem to undermine or block your ability to reach the goals you thought of in list one.

4. What are some possible things you could do to change these forces, without undermining the responsibilities you have to others? List those forces you feel you can change.

5. If you reach the objectives in list number one, will it make a good impact on the lives of others? Mark each of your objectives with a plus, for positive influence, or a minus, for a negative influence.

Do these goals you listed reflect a commitment to any of the following?

- Your own health and wholeness
- The development of your skills
- Making opportunity for others to develop skills
- Meeting the needs of others.

6. Assuming that you have discovered something about the difference between what you identify as your goals and priorities and what your behavior tells you, you may wish to consider the following suggestions.

- Identify an activity you would like to decrease in terms of time and energy investment. Be specific about what activity and the amount of time you would like to decrease.

- Identify an activity you would like to increase in importance, as measured in terms of time and energy invested. Be specific about what, how, and when.

- Use a daily log, calendar, or journal to begin the process of monitoring these two items for the next two weeks.

• Set a specific time each day to review these and your changing priorities. After each two-week period, identify another area of desired decrease and another of increase.

• If you find it difficult to maintain this commitment to changing your priorities, you may wish to consider the possibility of securing the help of your pastor, a brother or sister priest (someone with whom you have established a relationship of trust, under the covenant of God's grace). This person may help you sort out your goals and your barriers to reaching these goals.

• You may wish to find a prayer support group with a trusted group of people who are also committed to directing their ambitions after the mind of Christ. A Bible study and prayer support group is an effective way to enable us to realize our ambitions, including the ultimate ambition: to hear God say, "Well done good and faithful servant. You have been faithful over much."

Life's Possessions:

A Scene from Life

Bryan is burned out on helping the needy.

He has watched too many TV specials on starvation in Africa. And he has read too many letters from fund-raisers who want to help orphans.

At first, he tried to help. But the more he helped, the more he was coerced and downright "milked." Before long, he found himself helping so much it was beginning to affect his ability to pay the bills around the house.

One night, when the money ran out before the bills, Bryan and his wife decided to give nothing more than their tithe to the church. After all, they figured, the church uses some of that to help the needy.

Today, there are times when Bryan feels guilty about this decision. Like when he hears a late-night radio appeal for the needy, while he's resting on his "posture perfect" mattress. Or when he sees a commercial about the hungry, while he's sitting beneath the original oil painting in his living room.

But the clamor is too loud, and his wallet is too average. So respond he doesn't.

For the Bryan in us all, Al Truesdale has a few kind words.

Chapter 11

When Life's Possessions and Holy Living Clash

by Al Truesdale

Background Scripture: Matthew 6:24-34; 19:16-30

SARAH is a part-time employee of a Kansas City travel agency. She also conducts tours to other countries. One evening, she and I and other friends were being served in a restaurant. Sarah said to another friend, who is the wife of an anesthesiologist, "Susan, you should go along on our next shopping trip to Hong Kong."

I hoped she did not see my mouth drop open. A shopping trip to Hong Kong, China?

A few months earlier my wife and I were visiting missionaries in a Central American country. After a service in one church we were invited into the home of the pastor. We sat at a table in a room that served as living room, dining room, and Sunday School room. The furniture: a simple wooden table and chairs, and a refrigerator. We drank soft drinks and ate a tasty meat-filled cake. This represented sacrificial giving by the pastor to his guests. Beyond the open door I could see the flickering lights of scores of one- and two-room shanties, few with running water or electricity.

Some months before those two extremely different events, a star of the Kansas City Royals was negotiating a new contract. George Brett had rejected an offer reputed to be in the millions. Reason given? Not enough money. When asked by a *Kansas City Star* reporter, "When will you know that you have been offered enough?" Brett shot back, "You never have enough!"

Those three events have stuck in my memory. They seem to place in focus a problem not unique to either Sarah or

George Brett—the problem of materialism. But what is materialism? By what guidelines may a person be judged a materialist? Are there degrees of materialism? Can the average person in an industrialized nation escape materialism? Is our abundance of consumer goods and the ease with which most of us collect them incompatible with holy living? Is the holy life possible in a consumer society?

Holiness and materialism. What more difficult topic could we address? But why should it be difficult? No one says that materalism and living a holy life are compatible. Why not just condemn materialism, declare that we have nothing to do with it, and get on with our holy living?

Not so fast!

The problem is that most of us are plagued by this thing we so forcefully condemn. Furthermore, materialism is very difficult to define, and perhaps even more difficult to recognize in ourselves. One friend tried unsuccessfully to define materialism. Finally he threw up his hands and said half seriously, "I have it. A materialist is anyone who owns more than I do!"

Being able to define materialism is only part of the problem. Even if we define it, can we overcome it in our lives? Let's face it! These are not easy questions and there are no simple answers.

One way to try to define materialism is on the basis of how much a person owns. Looked at this way, materialism means owning more then we need. As soon as we take this route, the rich and super rich in Western Europe and North America come to mind. However, when we look more closely at this way of defining materialism, its dependability becomes less certain. At what point does a person own more than he needs? Can a person own a little more than he needs and not be a materialist? If so, how much more?

Some of Jesus' words seem to indicate that owning anything at all is equivalent to materialism. To one person who wanted to be a disciple, Jesus said, "If you want to be perfect, go, sell your possessions and give to the poor, and you will have treasure in heaven" (Matthew 19:21). To others Jesus said, "Any of you who does not give up everything he has cannot be my disciple" (Luke 14:33). Such instructions seem to rule out ownership of anything.

So if Jesus' words were taken literally, all of us would have to become wandering beggars. Family life and all forms of commerce and industry would be off-limits to Christians. Parents could not buy encyclopedias for their children, or provide places to shelter them. There could be no Christian school teachers, doctors, plumbers, or owners of business. All of these activities require ownership of at least some resources.

We know from reading the New Testament that some of Jesus' disciples continued to own fishing boats, and that Peter continued to own at least one house. We also know that Jesus borrowed a donkey from a disciple who owned it, and that Jesus was buried in a tomb that belonged to a "rich" disciple, Joseph of Arimathea.

Furthermore, Jesus told His disciples that they should live by faith in God alone. They should "take no thought" for their lives, what they would eat or what they would drink, or for their bodies as to what they would wear. Neither were they to worry about tomorrow. Taken literally, these words would mean that Christians could not buy health insurance, set educational goals for their children, or make plans for retirement.

But if Jesus' words are not to be taken literally, how much might a person own, and how much planning might one do, and still be a Christian? To these questions there are no pat answers. Even if we were to say that Christians should own only what they need, we would still not have helped ourselves very much. What does a person or a family *need*? Who could possibly answer this question? Does a family *need* a savings account? Does a child *need* to take piano lessons, or hold membership in the Scouts?

Furthermore, needs differ from one culture to another. *Needs* means one thing for a Nigerian farmer and something else for a stockbroker who lives on Long Island and commutes to Manhattan each working day.

The meaning of *needs,* or subsistence, differs even within a culture. Many parents think that children need to develop music appreciation and skills. So they spend good money, and rush through Saturday morning breakfast to get Becky to her piano lesson. Other families would see this as a misuse of money that could otherwise be used to feed hungry people. Many American families spend money to coordinate the furnishings in their homes. They match the colors in the carpets, furniture, and curtains. But many Amish families in Lancaster County, Pa., reject even carpets and curtains; these are considered obvious signs of materialistic extravagance. These Amish families use simple roll-up shades over their windows. Which estimate of needs is correct?

So, coming at materialism from the perspective of how much a person owns is no real help. It provides no absolute standard for defining materialism. Although there are many instances of extravagance and greed in our society, there is no universal standard of needs.

Another way to define materialism is in terms of a person's attitude toward what he owns or would like to own. Here "the material" includes physical objects of value, money, social status, one's race or sex, entertainment, and one's self-estimate.

As an attitude, materialism is the never-ending quest for abundance. It is characterized by a compulsion to acquire and accumulate material goods. This philosophy of life is often expressed in action even when it is verbally denied. Materialism is an attitude that says that life is made secure and valuable through material abundance. The more we own, the more complete life is.

Jesus once pointed to some Gentiles and said, look at them. Material things dominate their lives. Pursuit of the material drives them as a taskmaster drives a slave. Their days are spent in acquiring more and more goods (see Matthew 6:26-34).

In our day the disciples of materialism strain to amass money, buy a better house, own a fancier automobile, or take a more expensive vacation. Untiringly they furnish their homes and adorn themselves with things prescribed by the high priests of materialism—the ever-present advertisers who tell us what "real people" should own. Materialism is also embodied in corporations that make profit their only reason for existence—profit alone shapes their sales and social policies.

Materialism is a direct challenge to God's estimate of human life. Whereas the Bible teaches that people are created in His image and that they are most human when they love Him and people, materialism places the value of a person on what that person owns. Whereas the New Testament says that people should be viewed in light of the gospel of the kingdom of God, materialism sees people in light of their purchasing power. Materialism says that belonging to the "right race," the preferred social class, or living in the proper section of the city are the most important features of being human.

But materialism can never deliver what it promises. It promises freedom but delivers captivity. It promises security but breeds insecurity.

A while back in Kansas City, 83-year-old Mary Hudson, the owner of Hudson Oil, was convicted of tampering with the meters on the gasoline pumps of her service stations. She was among the most wealthy people in the United States. But driven by greed, she cheated her customers to increase her wealth.

Are there guidelines that can help people who sincerely want to live holy lives in a materialistic society? There are guidelines. But, there are no easy answers.

First, we should recognize there is no way on earth to equally distribute all the world's goods among people. We will always be painfully aware that while we are warm and well fed (and probably gaining weight), many people are hungry. This doesn't mean we approve of materialism or that we should rule out ways that seek to eliminate gross inequities. But it reminds us of a simple fact. And it keeps us from becoming emotionally and spiritually crippled by conditions that will never be totally eliminated. Some people have more because they have exploited others and some have less because they have been exploited. But it is also true that some have more because they have been good stewards of their resources, and some have less because they have been poor stewards. Such a statement may not satisfy the ideal, but it does agree with common sense.

Second, we must carefully examine the nature of our relationship to things. Am I driven by the desire to own material things? Do I act as though the best part of life is the accumulation of material goods? Holy living cannot thrive in an atmosphere charged with greed and anxiety over material acquisition.

A person cannot be governed by the Holy Spirit while at the same time serving the spirit of acquisition. Such slavery mocks one's hunger for the fruit of the Holy Spirit. We cannot be held captive to the gods of consumerism, and still be free to follow Jesus Christ. Admission of this for ourselves is a crucial first step.

Third, parents must examine the values they transmit to their children by their attitudes toward material possessions. Some children who hear materialism advocated all week long in the home find it difficult to see why their parents go to church on Sunday. As parents, we must model values that make possessions serve religious and human purposes.

Fourth, we should take a long, hard look at the way we evaluate people. Do we consider them more important if their clothing is stylish and expensive? Do we view them as having greater value because they are of the "right race" or "superior sex"? Do we seek the pleasure of their company just because of their social or ecclesiastical status? Mother Teresa of Calcutta said in New Orleans, "Never has the world been so hungry for love." She sees people through the eyes of Jesus. She values them as Jesus values people. One message in the ministry of Jesus is clear: people were more important to Him than were status, possessions, and institutions.

Fifth, we should examine our spending habits. Do I feel compelled to "own the best and the latest"? If so, what drives me to adopt this philosophy?

Many people so commit their resources to endless shopping sprees that they find it both impossible and unattractive to give liberally to relieve world hunger, to support community relief projects, to help orphans, or to assist the church.

Sixth, we should learn about the extent of poverty in the world and how the extravagance of some countries contributes to poverty in many developing countries. We Americans, for example, consume 30 percent of the world's resources, but we represent only 6 percent of the world's population.

There are many books that can explain the economic and environmental interdependence among nations, and they can help Christians develop more simple life-styles. A few of these books are: *Rich Christians in an Age of Hunger,* by Ron Sider; *Freedom of Simplicity,* by Richard Foster; and *World Hunger: Ten Myths,* by Frances Moore Lappe.

Finally, all of us must be careful students of the New Testament. Its repeated instructions regarding godliness ought to shape all our values. In Titus we read, "For the grace of God has dawned upon the world with healing for all mankind; and by it we are disciplined to renounce godless ways and worldly desires, and to live a life of temperance, honesty, and godliness in the present age" (Titus 2:11-12, NEB).

Integrity:

A Scene from Life

Brad works as editor for a Christian charitable organization that makes its money through direct-mail solicitation, mostly from older folk.

"For $15.00 a month you can clothe, feed, and educate a little orphan." You've read the letters and seen the ads.

Two months ago, the organization hired a secular company to help them with the fund-raising. "Crises," the consultant said. "That's what you need. The more crises you have, the more money you'll raise."

The organization soon found itself creating crises out of thin air. Each month they'd meet with their consultant to decide what would go in the next appeal letter. And discussion would go something like this. "Let's say the director of the Holy Land orphanage called the charity president here in the States (which he didn't). They need a new boiler for hot water, so let's have the director say the old one's ready to blow up" (which it isn't).

Though Brad doesn't take part in this conniving, he feels guilty by association. For Brad, and for other Christians, Millard Reed tells how to survive in the real world without sacrificing integrity.

Chapter 12

Can Integrity Survive in a Cruel, Hard World?

by Millard C. Reed

Background Scripture: Exodus 20:3-17; Matthew 7:7-12

IMAGINE that the name of the new pastor has just been announced, and it is your name. You are the new pastor. A smiling, receptive people embrace you with holy love, await your inspired preaching from the Word, and seek counsel in matters of practical living.

As their pastor you will not enjoy the luxury of the theoretical setting, as a college professor of ethics might. Even if you could give your people clear theories, they will want more than theories. They will want to know what they ought to do in specific situations, and some of those situations will be complicated beyond imagination. Here are some real-life situations, with only the names changed and the settings altered slightly.

Setting No. 1

Ron and his wife and two teenage children moved to your town a month ago. He is in his mid-40s and is an able comptroller. It was a personal matter that prompted the move, but Ron had no trouble getting work in your city. He is now comptroller of a large manufacturing plant and doing well. On Wednesday night he asks to talk to you.

"I can't believe it!" Ron begins, "I haven't even told my wife yet. But today the president of the company came by my office to commend me on the good work I am doing. Then he explained that it would be necessary for me to maintain two sets of books, one for the IRS and one that would be maintained as private files. He explained that the company had followed this pattern for many years and that he depended on me to carry out the policy of the company.

"Pastor, I don't feel I can do that. On the other hand, if I quit and report the company to the IRS there would be a court case and either they or I would be discredited. If I simply quit without reporting it, I might have a difficult time getting another job with equal pay. Pastor, what should I do?"

Setting No. 2

Julie's mother suggests that you drop by to see her daughter. She has seemed depressed since John left four months ago on a six-month overseas business assignment. As pastor, you are more than happy to drop by, for Julie was reared in the church, was active in the youth department, and is now the mother of a two-year-old.

After a polite conversation, Julie breaks down and confides in you that while John has been away, an illicit affair has developed with her boss and she is pregnant by him.

"I know you think abortion is wrong, but if John finds out about this our marriage is over. Pastor, what can I do?"

Setting No. 3

Jim had managed a service station for some years and was very capable as a mechanic. So when the local auto dealership offered him a job as manager of the service department, with a sizable increase in salary, he jumped at it. At last he had hours that were reasonable and an income that could provide for his family. When the new warranty policy came through from the manufacturer, the owner of the dealership explained to Jim that he would not announce this to the customers. This way, the dealership could collect from both the manufacturer and the customers for service rendered. "It's the only way we can be competitive," explained the owner. "I am sure you understand."

As the others had done, Jim comes to you and asks, "What should I do?"

Setting No. 4

Jerry is emotionally unstable. He is often a seeker at the altar. He married too soon and is now just 24. In the seclusion of the pastor's study, he confesses that for some months he has been spending an occasional night with a girlfriend. Now he is perplexed. In the same month both his wife and his girlfriend tell him they are pregnant. "I love my wife, Janice, but I love Carrie too," he whines. "Pastor, what should I do?"

Setting No. 5

Dan was just gloriously saved—a radical change from a life of sin. He is ecstatic in his new faith and wants to tell everyone about the difference Jesus has made in his life. About three weeks into his new faith he makes an appointment with you, his pastor. He explains that as an insurance agent he falsified papers in his favor to the effect that the mother company sent him $20,000 more than he had a legitimate right to. "Pastor, if I confess, I will probably be sent to jail. At least I will lose my job. I don't have the money to make the restitution. What should I do?"

As Pastor, You Must Respond

If you are the pastor, how would you answer the sincere questions of your people?

Because of the current emphasis on individual freedom, many have concluded we should not make moral judgments on others. Philosophers like Bertrand Russell say such moralizing is "a certain wish." So, "Let every man be a law unto himself," has been construed to mean there are no "rights" and no "wrongs" except as they are judged by individuals. "Dos and don'ts" imposed by any judge have become very unpopular. The most that many advisors are willing to say these days is, "Let your conscience be your guide."

But the people who come to their pastor bring a Christian conscience with them. Their moral crisis does not spring from a lack of moral duty, but from a conflict of moral duties.

Since they share moral values with their pastor they come to him to hear what he thinks. But they're also concerned about what the fellowship thinks, what the Scripture says, and what God says about the critical decision. The situation is not theoretical. They must act. They must act soon. They sincerely want help from society, Scripture, their spiritual leader, and God.

Moral Issues

The pastor is not without resources by which to make moral judgments. Scripture and ethical history provide many aids. The Scriptures provide the greatest of all resources for guidance in moral decision making. The Ten Commandments, although it is a list of "dos and don'ts," still provide the foundation of all moral reflection. The first four have to do with our relationship to God; and they demand we have reverence for His name and His day. The fifth calls us to respect our parents. The last five are all stated in the negative and have to do with interpersonal relationships. "You shall not murder. You shall not commit adultery. You shall not steal. You shall not give false testimony . . . You shall not covet" (Exodus 20:13-17).

Many moral problems would be resolved by the careful and prayerful application of these great commandments.

As the greatest teacher of the law, Jesus made it clear that He did not come to abolish the law or the prophets, but to fulfill them. His teaching fulfilled the law by applying it to "internal" as well as "external" ethical situations. He made it clear that hatred or "mental murder" is as wrong as murder. Mental adultery, or lust, is as much a violation of the law as is the act itself. Jesus forever exposed the Pharisees who judged the sinner harshly but who committed the same sin in their hearts.

Jesus also summarized the Mosaic code with statements about love. When a teacher of the law asked which was the greatest commandment, Jesus answered, "'Hear, O Israel, the Lord our God, the Lord is one. Love the Lord your God with all your heart and with all your soul and with all your mind and with all your strength.' The second is this: 'Love your neighbor as yourself.' There is no commandment greater than these" (Mark 12:28-31). The Golden Rule from the teachings of Jesus is, "Do to others what you would have them do to you" (Matthew 7:12).

Although the commandments of Moses, as interpreted by our Lord's insight of love, provide the great foundation for application of the Scripture to practical ethical questions, there are also aids from the New Testament writers. Paul, for example, provides a helpful base for situations related to the care and use of the body when he speaks of it as "a temple of the Holy Spirit" (1 Corinthians 6:19). James' Epistle focuses on the moral obligation we have to provide for a needy brother or sister. Peter has counsel for both husband and wife in matters of conduct. He even offers some beauty hints.

Our primary resource and guidebook, then, is the Holy Scripture. It provides a series of time-tested fundamentals by which we may judge the proposed options and make a sound decision.

Not all situations lend themselves to the authoritarian word of Scripture easily, however. All Scripture is subject to interpretation, and wise men of the centuries have drawn various philosophical conclusions.

Outside the frame of Scripture, the learned Socrates (470-399 B.C.), "patron saint" of moral philosophers, made three negative conclusions: (1) We ought not judge on the basis of emotions. (2) We ought not go by what people generally think. (They could be wrong.) (3) We ought never do what is morally wrong.[1] He also submits a threefold ethical guide that carries the spirit of the Ten Commandments. It goes as follows: (1) We ought never to harm anyone. (2) We ought to keep our promises. (3) We ought to obey and respect our parents and teachers.[2]

Aristotle (384-322 B.C.) was a disciple of Socrates and concluded that all pertinent facts, theories, and opinions must be compared in order to sift out the truth in a moral question. Let me briefly mention two other philosophers of ancient times. Epicurus (341-270 B.C.) viewed the absence of pain in the body and of trouble in the soul as the ultimate good. Zeno of Citium (336-264 B.C.), leader of Stoicism, concluded that man's end is to live virtuously.

The Christian era has included many interpreters. I will mention two. Augustine (354-430 A.D.) observed that man's happiness is the ultimate end, but that it can be found only in God. Susanna Wesley (1662-1735) gave this counsel to her famous sons, John and Charles Wesley: Whatever weakens your reason, impairs the tenderness of your conscience, obscures

117

your sense of God, or takes off the relish of spiritual things, whatever increases the authority of your body over your mind, that thing for you is sin.

In modern times, bodies of believers have conscientiously sought out guidelines based on biblical interpretation and have laid them down in "disciplines" or "manuals." These represent the combined judgment of godly men and women, which, while not accepted as an absolute authority as is the Scripture, ought to be maintained as a guideline in conscientious decision making.

So while the pastor is confronted with tough ethical questions, he is not without resources for dealing with them.

How do these resources bear upon these particular ethical questions?

This is the great practical question. Theoretical answers to theoretical questions will not do. Let's return to the pastoral settings with which this chapter began and see how one pastor made application and how real people responded. Be prepared to carry on the exercise with settings from your own life, when the list in the book is exhausted.

Setting No. 1

When Ron looked at the scriptural command: "You shall not give false testimony," he concluded that he could not comply with his boss's request. He quit his job, then found it difficult to locate another one. So after an extended time of financial stress, Ron gave up his career, returned to the Northeast and began farming again as his family had done for generations. Some would say that Ron made the wrong choice. He does not think so.

Setting No. 2

Julie and the pastor looked at the command of scripture regarding murder. She shared the pastor's judgment that abortion is wrong. Programs of adoption were discussed. Even so, Julie felt she could not give birth to the baby, though she knew it was the "right thing." She had an abortion. Her husband never knew. They are happily married today. Julie suffers stomach pains and times of depression.

Setting No. 3

Jim placed the proposal of his boss under the judgment of the Ten Commandments. When he told his boss he could not do as the company demanded, he was fired. For a period of time, life looked bleak. Unemployment lasted several months. Finally, a company seeking a factory representative heard of Jim's skill and history. Jim was hired with the comment that their factory was looking for a man with just the kind of hard-nosed integrity that Jim had demonstrated. His decision was, and continues to be, a great benefit—financially and in other ways—for Jim and his family.

Setting No. 4

There was no easy option for Jerry. His marriage vows, though sacred, had already been violated. His pastor admonished him to return to his lawful wife and provide financially for the child his girlfriend was carrying. Jerry did not heed the counsel of his pastor. He divorced his wife, abandoned his child by her, and married his girlfriend. They are still married today. A few years later, his former wife found a good Christian man who became her husband; they are in the fellowship of the church.

Setting No. 5

Dan knew instinctively from the beginning that his act was theft, and it was wrong. His question had more to do with a course of action in the light of the wrong. After a lot of prayer with the pastor, he decided he must make restitution. He declined the pastor's offer to accompany him. Dan was fired. Only with the promise of full restitution did he avoid legal entanglements. He is paying off the debt, with interest, over the next 10 years.

These are not storybook endings. But in each case they represent actual people grappling with real situations in the light of the judgments of God and the centuries of human struggles with moral judgments.

Had you been pastor, what would you have counseled?

---

1. Plato's *Crito* as quoted in William K. Frankena, *Ethics* (Englewood Cliffs, N.J.: Prentice-Hall, Inc., 1973), 2.
2. Ibid.

Holiness at Work:

A Scene from Life

Jennifer is a divorced lady with two boys: a young teenage invalid who lives in a wheelchair, and a lazy high school graduate who is as helpful around the house as termites.

Jennifer is not a Christian, but her neighbor, Steve, is.

Steve keeps his yard looking immaculate. Jennifer has not the time, energy, or interest for cutting her lawn. And the closest her older son comes to grooming the weed patch is when he combs his hair.

It's now two months into the growing season, and Jennifer's lawn is approaching three feet high in places—two feet over what the city allows.

"I didn't know she was going to let it get this high," Steve said, "or I would have cut it for her. But now it's too high for my mower."

What should Steve do, buy a six-foot high privacy fence, or write city hall a compassionate note and ask if a city employee could come out and eat a yard of weeds at Jennifer's expense?

Putting holiness into action is not always as easy as playing Monopoly. You don't always know what to do next.

In "Holiness in the Marketplace" Gene Van Note tells a moving story that illustrates this truth: Whenever you are in doubt about what to do, you should do the loving thing.

Chapter 13

Holiness in the Marketplace

by Gene Van Note

Background Scripture: Luke 10:30-37; 1 Corinthians 12:4-11

OKIE PEERED anxiously out the window of the Delta Air Lines passenger jet as it landed at the airport in Charlotte, N.C.

Everything looked strange. But then, she had not expected to recognize anything. She was half a world away from the country of her birth. Never before in her 23 years had she traveled outside her Korean homeland. International air travel was an impossible dream, not an occasional luxury for Korean families like hers.

But here she was. As the children used to shout when they played hide-and-seek, "Here I am, ready or not!"

Along with the other passengers, Okie hustled out of the plane into the airport lobby. Caught in the crush of family reunions and businessmen meeting clients, she could not see if there was someone there to greet her. The "big" Americans seemed to engulf her. Like most of her countrymen, Okie is small. Actually, smaller than most, she is a tiny 4 feet 8 inches in height.

The tiny Korean traveler moved to the edge of the crowd. Her eyes darted from face to face. There was no need to try to read the signs. That was impossible. She did not understand English. She was confident, however, that the one American she knew, would be there. She had met him in Korea. He had promised to love her "till death do us part."

Surely her soldier-husband was in the milling crowd—somewhere. Okie kept looking. When the crowd thinned out, she walked to one end of the terminal, then to the other. Always looking—hoping to see that one friendly face.

But they were all strangers—all busy. Every one of them was speaking some language that had such funny sounds.

121

Okie returned to the gate where she had exited the plane. The lobby was empty. Only an occasional person walked quickly past, toward an unknown destination.

She sat down. Gradually it dawned on her that her husband was not coming.

Anxiety was replaced with fear. Now what would she do?

She waited and thought and might have cried if she hadn't been so tired. Okie had been traveling nonstop for almost 24 hours.

Bill Tate was on duty as ground supervisor for Delta Air Lines in Charlotte when Okie's plane landed. An airlines supervisor has a major responsibility while a plane is on the ground. The needs of the plane, its cargo, and its passengers are all referred to him.

Especially the difficult and insoluble problems.

Thus it was that Bill learned about a war bride named Okie. But when he met her, he did not know that she was expecting to meet a soldier-husband. Her passport simply identified her as a Korean. It was immediately evident that she spoke no English. Since neither he nor anyone else in the terminal knew Okie's native tongue, communication was nearly impossible.

During his years as a supervisor with Delta, Bill had encountered every conceivable emergency. He knew where to turn for immediate help and long-range assistance. He often took advantage of those social services designed to aid weary travelers. On many occasions he had referred confused or troubled passengers to them. They were caring people, but usually very busy. Without weighing the immediate cost or long-term implications, Bill made a quick decision that was in keeping with his Christian faith. He knew that he could not go to his comfortable home at the end of his shift and entrust Okie to an overworked welfare agency. She was too vulnerable—too alone.

When he made the decision to take her home for the night, he never doubted that his wife, Barbara, would respond just as he had. He was right, of course. Barbara urged him to bring Okie as quickly as possible. When Bill hung up the phone, he glanced at his desk calendar. The date was November 16, 1976.

Under different circumstances, Bill and Okie would have been a comical sight as they came through the door. Slender and tall at six feet four inches, Bill towered almost two feet above the slight little lady from the East.

But Barbara did not laugh, though she did manage a bit of a smile. The panic in Okie's face caught her attention.

"She just stood there . . . trembling. I looked into her eyes. They were filled with fear. She was so tired and so scared. I said, 'Hello,' but she didn't answer. I guess she just didn't know what the word meant."

Then Barbara did something that no man, regardless of his efficiency or compassion, could do. She opened her arms and Okie ran to her.

Volumes of love were communicated by that tender touch. Okie knew that she had found a friend. But that was about all anyone knew at that moment. It would be days before they began to understand the story and weeks before the problem began to be resolved. It will take eternity to measure the wide-reaching implications of the experience.

It was immediately evident, however, that the Tates were woefully unprepared for the challenge of having this little Korean as their houseguest. While Barbara waited for them to arrive from the airport, she decided she would prepare herself for the encounter. She turned in the encyclopedia to "Korea." Her primary concern was to cook some food that Okie would like. All it said was that Koreans eat lots of rice. It was weeks before she learned that Koreans prepare it much differently than she did for her family.

Customs, culture, food, language—these were just some of the challenges presented by their unexpected visitor.

Money was another factor. Bill had a good salary with Delta Air Lines. But he already had the needs of three children to meet: two teenagers, Steve and Beverly, and an active six-year-old named Scott.

There was another very obvious problem—Okie was seven and one-half months pregnant.

In fact, this is what had brought her on her flight into the unknown. Children with American GI fathers have no future in

Korea. They have absolutely no civil rights. These mixed-race children cannot attend public school, are denied even the most menial jobs in a factory, cannot join the military, or even apply for employment with the government. They are outcasts.

Okie's pregnancy was complicated by yet another fact. International air lines have rules restricting the flight of expectant mothers after they reach their eighth month of pregnancy.

There had been some indications that her husband, Larry, planned to bring her to the United States as soon as he could work it out. Far away in Korea there was no way to know that Larry was doing his best, especially in light of the obstacles he had encountered when he returned home. No one among his family and friends looked with favor at the idea of a Korean war bride becoming a part of their community. Larry was discouraged. He was learning that these things take time.

But Okie could not wait.

No loving family wants their child to move hundreds of thousands of miles away with the full knowledge that they would never see them again. However, when they looked around and saw what was happening to the half-breed children on the streets, they knew they had no choice. Okie must go to America—immediately. If only they had the money.

An older sister came up with the answer. She and her husband had borrowed money to purchase a piece of property near Seoul. Without asking her husband for approval, she took Okie downtown to the office of Korean Air Lines. There they bought a ticket for Charlotte, N.C., where Okie thought Larry was living.

But Larry was not there. He picked up his mail in a little town several hundred miles away, where his parents lived.

After Okie had been living with the Tates for some time, a reporter for the *Charlotte Observer* heard about the experience. His front-page story recounted the details, giving special attention to the compassionate involvement of Bill and Barbara Tate. He said nothing about the extra financial pressure the family was feeling. However, his readers were able to read between the lines. Unsolicited offers of help began to flood the newspaper. Soon, Okie's needs were adequately met.

The people of Charlotte wanted to do far more than this, however. When they learned that the recently discharged soldier had not been able to find employment, there were many job offers. A house was offered at low rent to aid the young couple. While these experiences of kindness kept coming, an aggressive reporter discovered where Larry was living. He was overwhelmed by the way the Charlotte community had rallied to help him and Okie. Thus it was that after many weeks, a frightened Korean war bride was reunited with her husband. Together they began the tough task of building a happy home.

Fortunately, they were not alone. Bill and Barbara Tate and their children are all dedicated Christians. The little mother-to-be who had entered their life without warning had left quite an impact on them. They continued to be involved with Larry and Okie. Their nonaccusing acceptance made it easier for Larry to weather the notoriety and publicity. Larry and Okie became a part of their circle of friends. And for the Tates, that meant the church.

Bill and Barbara are happy activists in the Church of the Nazarene. At the present time, he is a lay member of the District Advisory Board and was one of the delegates from the North Carolina District to the 1985 General Assembly. In recent years, Barbara has become deeply involved in children's ministries, not only in the local church, but also in teachers' workshops throughout the area.

Yet, in spite of all their Christian involvement in outside projects, the Tates are primarily interested in their local church. They were pleasantly committed to the Thomasboro Church of the Nazarene when it became clear that First Church in Charlotte was going through a period of intense crisis. Characteristically, when they were assured that it was the leading of the Lord, they left their comfortable church for hard work on the religious frontier.

The Tates were still attending the Thomasboro church when Okie arrived. It was a normal expression of their love and faith for them to invite the young couple to be a part of their

Christian fellowship. Thus, a great many people shared the joy the Sunday Larry and Okie asked Jesus Christ to become the Lord of their lives.

The North Carolina Korean community responded with overflowing gratitude when the story became public. They could hardly believe that an unknown white couple would be so kind to a vulnerable Oriental. Later on, they invited the Tates to a special dinner.

"They treated us like royalty," Barbara remembers, "but we came back home to dirty dishes!" Ah yes, but you can always come home to dirty dishes for far less meaningful reasons.

Partly as a result of the news coverage, a Korean church was organized. The only "white American" dignitaries invited to the first service were Bill and Barbara Tate.

United Press International picked up the story and distributed it on its national news line. Soon the Tates were receiving letters of appreciation from a great many grateful Koreans, especially in the eastern United States. Even now, several years later, they receive Christmas cards from Koreans they have never met. Among them is a Christian Korean who lives in Cincinnati, Ohio, who phones occasionally just to keep in touch. The Tates have made a great many new friends.

Okie's family was delighted, also. When they finally learned what had happened, the sister wrote Barbara. It cost the sister $32.00 in U.S. money to have the letter translated into English and typed. "It was such a lovely letter," Barbara remembers happily.

But it was not all easy. There were also ugly letters, filled with hostility and prejudice. Not everyone approved of the out-flowing of love to a racially mixed couple. It was not easy to sleep at night after one of these messages of hate arrived.

There were many happy, and some quite humorous, experiences while Okie was living with the Tates. But at times it was emotionally exhausting. The pressure of the harsh letters and the drain of being compassionate was taking its toll.

"One night," Barbara recalls, "I had finally reached the end. I asked, 'Lord, are we into something we can't get out of?'"

"Within a few hours, the answer came. It became clear that

this was not an unplanned event. It didn't just happen that Bill was on duty when Okie's plane arrived. She was in our home by appointment, not accident."

Barbara continues, "We have learned so much from being with Okie. Everyone in the family has learned to be more sensitive to the people who pass our way. We've learned that we are here under appointment to say something for the Lord. We'll never be the same. Nor do we want to be."

The passing of the years has caused the families to drift apart. They attend different churches now and live in widely separated parts of Charlotte. They see each other only occasionally, and perhaps that is the way it should be. It allows Larry and Okie to continue to grow. But the friendship continues. Just recently when Barbara answered the phone, Okie was on the other end of the line. Before their conversation was completed, Okie told her, "Mom, I pray every day, 'Make me a good woman.'"

Bill's unplanned response to a person in need resulted in months of compassionate involvement and an ever-widening circle of ministry. It is a beautiful example of holy love in action.

From *Holiness in the Marketplace,* by Gene Van Note. Copyright 1981 by Beacon Hill Press of Kansas City, Kansas City, Mo. Used by permission.

Other Dialog Series Books

For a description of all available Dialog Series books, including some that may not be listed here, contact your publishing house and ask for the free Dialog Series brochure.